SUPREME® BAR REVIEW

Criminal Law

Bar Exam Review

Supreme Bar Review
30539 Pinetree Road, Suite 224
Cleveland, Ohio 44124

(866) BAR-PREP (toll-free)

SupremeBarReview.com

Printed in the United States of America.

ISBN-13: 978-1-936450-03-9

This book is intended as a general review of legal subjects. It is not intended as a source of advice for the solution of legal matters or problems. For advice on legal matters, the reader should consult an attorney.

For information address:

Supreme Bar Review
30539 Pinetree Road, Suite 224
Cleveland, Ohio 44124

SupremeBarReview.com

TABLE OF CONTENTS

I. ELEMENTS OF CRIMINAL LIABILITY

In general, three components are required for criminal liability: (1) *actus reus*, (2) *mens rea*, and (3) causation (for those crimes that require a particular result).

A. ACTUS REUS

Actus Reus can be a voluntary physical act (act of commission) or a failure to act where the defendant is under a legal duty to act (act of omission).

1. Acts of Commission

In order to impose criminal liability, the common law required proof of an *actus reus* or "criminal act". *Actus reus* is a legal term of art, which addresses volitional action. The classic definition of *actus reus* is that it is a controlled movement, *i.e.*, a willed movement or intentional act. The criminal act is said to express the evil intent of the criminal actor and provide concrete evidence of the intent to do harm.

Watch Out!

Crimes which are good test fodder for *actus reus*.
Possession crimes (mere possession versus active possession), status crimes (being drunk), and inchoate (anticipatory or incomplete) crimes are controversial in litigation as having the barest semblance of an *actus reus.*

Example: Active possession distinguished from inactive possession: A drug dealer who leaves an undisplayed gun in his pocket during an illegal drug transaction, does not actively "use" the weapon during the commission of a crime and therefore may be guilty of drug trafficking, but not the sentence enhancing greater offense of committing a crime with the use of a firearm.

Watch Out!

Behavioral conditions which are good test fodder for *actus reus*.
The underlying notion at common law and retained in the MPC § 2.01 is that acts over which one lacks control cannot serve as *actus reus* for the simple reason that uncontrolled acts cannot support a logical inference about intent. It is possible for movement to occur absent volitional thinking, such as reflex, unconsciousness, or automatism. However, such movements would not qualify as an *actus reus* because no inference about evil intent may be inferred from them.

Example: Sleepwalking is increasingly becoming a valid defense in the majority of American jurisdictions. If A, while sleepwalking, attacks B, A's action may fall short of criminal liability because it occurred lacking conscious thought or was not the product of the actor's will.

2. **Acts of Omission**

As a general rule, there is no liability for omissions to act. Society imposes the burden of self-care on individuals, and not on another. The general rule of non-liability for omissions serves to impose strict liability on victims to bear the consequences of their own misfortune.

a. **Supporting rationales for the common law rule are as follows:**

1) Non-liability for omissions deters would-be victims from taking risks which would otherwise jeopardize their own safety.

2) In a heterogeneous society achieving uniformity as to which moral obligations to enforce by the criminal sanction is unlikely.

3) Requirements to intervene at the risk of criminal sanction is a derogation of liberty.

b. **Exception: duty of care and ability to act.** However, the common law allowed for omissions, *i.e.,* the failure to act could be the basis for the imposition of criminal liability under limited circumstances. Those limited circumstances required a pre-existing duty imposed by law or custom to act, and an ability to act under the given circumstances. Thus, the traditional exceptions to the general rule of non-liability for omissions are limited to situations where it is appropriate to relieve the victim from the burden of self-care, *e.g.*, a baby or an incapacitated spouse.

The following are common law duties:

1) duty based on relationship,

2) duty based on statute,

3) duty based on contract,

4) duty based on voluntary assumption of care,

5) duty based upon the creation of peril, and

6) duty to control the conduct of others.

Example: parent's duty to a child: A mother may be liable as an accomplice to child endangering, if she does not intervene to prevent her boyfriend from molesting her daughter (duty based on relationship).

Example: voluntary assumption of care: The existence of a prior relationship where an otherwise capable person assumes a risk in reliance upon another may also serve to make an omission relevant under a theory of detrimental reliance. If a disabled mother of two adult daughters lives with one daughter, but not the other, the daughter who lives with her mother may be held to have assumed the duty of care for her ailing mother in the sense that had the daughter not taken the position of caretaker, other help in the form of the state welfare agency would have provided for the ailing adult (duty based on voluntary assumption of care).

c. **Supporting rationale for imposing a duty of care to act:** The common law thus recognized a duty to aid under such limited circumstances as where the presumption for self-care is untenable and the assignment of a duty to help is necessary to support key social arrangements as in the care of parents for small children or invalid adult family members. However, duty of care had to be coupled with an ability to act. A parent who cannot swim is not required to jump in the lake to rescue a drowning child.

MBE Advice

The MBE recently tested the duty placed on an individual to act when one of three participants was committing a crime which the other two individuals had no prior knowledge of and did not assist in any way. This MBE scenario tested the criminal liability of the non-participants.

As a general rule, mere presence is not enough to impose criminal liability. Remember, without a specific duty imposed by common law or statute, a person may sit idly by and watch something as heinous as a murder occur with no criminal liability.

B. MENS REA

Mens Rea is the intent or state of mind of the defendant that must exist while committing an *actus reus* in order for defendant to be guilty of a particular crime. With the exception of a small category of "strict liability crimes", in order for a defendant to be considered guilty of a crime, the defendant's criminal action must be coupled with a "guilty mind". Both the mental and physical elements must co-exist.

1. The guilty mind

Mens rea is a legal term of art, which refers to the subjective state of mind. It is the subjective mind, which upon due deliberation motivates the criminal act. The criminal operation of the subjective mind has long been the basis for imposing the penal sanction at common law, and this is especially so under the Model Penal Code.

2. **Terminology**
Although the existence of moral culpability is what primarily distinguishes a crime from an intentional tort or an intentional breach of a contractual duty, the more precise and consistently understood terminology of the MPC dominates modern criminal statutory schemes. Bear in mind that distinctions in mental states only have functional meaning in terms of the gravity of the offense charged and thus the severity of the sentence following conviction.

a. **Common law terms.** First, due to the influence of canon courts in the early Middle Ages, *mens rea* or scienter referred to the evilness or "actual wickedness" of the actor. Second, in an effort to avoid the vagueness of morally laden terminology, early statutory formulations of *mens rea* focused on the actor's criminal intent and expressed *mens rea* in terms of either general intent or specific intent.

1) **General Intent Crimes:** General intent spoke to harm caused by an actor's breach of baseline behavioral norms. General intent is often used in the same way that criminal intent is used to describe the actor's criminal purpose or *mens rea*. General intent is commonly understood as the intent necessary for committing the *actus reus* of the offense.

2) **Specific Intent Crimes:** Specific intent spoke of an actor's primary objective in terms of committing a future act (*e.g.,* Burglary is the breaking and entering of another's dwelling house with the intent to commit a felony therein), having a special motive (*e.g.,* Larceny is the taking and carrying away of another's personal property with the intent to steal), or knowledge of attendant circumstances (*e.g.,* Receiving stolen property with knowledge that it was stolen).

3) **Attempts**: All attempt crimes are specific intent crimes, regardless that the underlying offense may have been a general intent crime.

Examples: Common law examples of crimes requiring specific intent include: larceny ("with the intent to steal") and burglary ("with the intent to commit a felony therein").

3. **Model Penal Code terms**
Because the specific intent-general intent dichotomy stretched too broadly, MPC § 2.02 re-formulated *mens rea* in terms of the actor's awareness as to the nature the conduct, likelihood of harm, or existence of a law proscribing the conduct or harmful result. The MPC identifies four criminal states of mind: purpose, knowing, reckless, and negligent.

1) **Purposeful behavior:** It is the conscious object of the criminal actor to bring about a result.

   Example: A plants a bomb in B's office. A's sole aim is to kill B. A commits a purposeful killing of B.

2) **Knowing behavior:** It is practically certain that a result will occur.

   Example: If A plants the bomb knowing that due to her proximity to B, the bomb will also kill B's secretary, A commits a knowing killing of B's secretary even though she was not the object of the act.

3) **Reckless behavior:** The criminal actor is aware of and disregards a substantial and unjustifiable risk (advertent). Disregard of the risk constitutes a gross deviation from the standard of a law-abiding person.

   Example: If the possible proximity of the janitor making his rounds places him in jeopardy, A's disregard of a known risk constitutes a reckless killing of the janitor.

4) **Negligent behavior:** The criminal actor should have been aware of a substantial and unjustifiable risk (inadvertent). Failure to perceive the risk constitutes a gross deviation from the standard of a reasonable person.

   Example: If A places the bomb in the office basement to avoid killing the secretary and the janitor, but where there is evidence from which a reasonable person should infer the occasional presence of a hobo, A's disregard of a risk that he should have known constitutes a negligent killing.

4. **Differentiated mental states for different elements of the same crime**
   In a Model Penal Code jurisdiction, each element of the statutory crime may be assigned a different *mens rea* proof requirement.

   Example: The crime of assault on a police officer requires a showing that an assault occurred, but there is no requirement to show that the attacker knew the victim's status as a police officer.

5. **The doctrine of transferred intent**
   Sometimes an actor intending to cause a particular harm actually accomplishes a different harm. The criminal law addresses this inadvertent divorce by marrying the intent of the actor (*mens rea)* with the harm act actually done by the actor (*actus reus)* to construct a composite crime. The rationale behind this doctrine is that defendant's offensive act though it did not accomplish its intended purpose, may be viewed as a general wrong against the whole world, which only by happenstance wreaked harm upon the victim who was in the wrong place at the

wrong time. Thus, the doctrine of transferred intent is more aptly described as a marriage of intent with an act rather than a transfer.

Note: Some commentators believe that the doctrine of transferred intent is not necessary. Suppose A aims at B intending to kill B, but hits and kills C. Here, commentators suggest, it is only necessary that A have the intent to kill a person (not necessarily a specific person) and cause that person's death to be guilty of murder.

Example: Defendant A intends to kill B. A knows that B takes his lunch break at the same time everyday and promptly leaves his office at 11:55 A.M.. A decides he will run over B with his automobile when B takes his lunch break. A goes to the office building and waits in his car. At 11:54 A.M., A guns his car towards the door and mistakenly runs over and kills C, who exited the building and decided to take an early lunch that day. Due to the doctrine of transferred intent, A is liable for the deliberate killing of C, whom he never intended to kill. The intent to kill *(mens rea)* is merged with the actual killing of C *(actus reus)* to form a crime. If malice aforethought is found at the time of the killing, even if a third party is killed rather than the intended victim, the defendant is guilty of murder.

a. **Intent may be polygamous,** *i.e.,* a single intent may be married to several harmful results to numerous unintended victims. If A shoots into a crowd with the intent to injure B, A's intent would be married to injuries to all others as well as all property damage caused by the shot.

b. **Intent across different states of *mens rea.*** The doctrine of transferred intent also applies across different states of *mens rea.* A specific intent may be married down to a general intent harmful result to construct a composite general intent crime but generally not the other way around. A small minority view would allow a general intent to marry up to a specific intent criminal/act to construct a composite specific intent crime.

   Example: An actor who fired a shot, intending to kill B, misses and injures C would be liable for an attempted murder against B, but only an aggravated battery against C.

   Example: The minority view of transferred intent allows a mental state to be upgraded or married up to fit the *actus reus.* For example, A shot at B, only intending to warn him, *i.e.,* reckless endangerment (general intent crime). However, A's gunshot hit B and B subsequently died. A would be liable for murder even though he never intended to kill B. The marriage up or upgrade in mental state is problematic because it allows for a higher level of punishment than was actually formed by the shooter. The shooter will be punished for an intent or criminal mentality that he never formed.

6. **The reasonable person standards**
The "reasonable person" is a legal standard by which the exercise of due care and vigilance is evaluated in torts and the existence of moral culpability is evaluated in the law of crimes. The law measures moral culpability by two quite distinct standards: objective reasonableness and subjective reasonableness.

   a. **The objective standard.** The objectively reasonable person standard assumes a population with baseline commonalities of knowledge, human capability, and societal values.

      Example: A driver approaching an intersection is presumed to know the meaning of stop signs or the rules of the road; to be mentally and physically capable (able to comprehend the speed of oncoming traffic and to see and act with at least common dexterity in the operation of the vehicle); and to make judgments consistent with societal values (*e.g.*, prioritize risk to human life over being late for work).

   b. **The subjective standard.** The subjectively reasonable person standard voids the baseline or community standards in favor of individualized standards.

      Example: Assume A is defending against a charge of involuntary manslaughter stemming from a criminally negligent car accident. A's objective defense might be that traffic conditions were risky generally. A's subjective defense would be that his road rage led him to take risks that an ordinary reasonable person would not have taken.

7. **Strict Liability**
Under very limited circumstances, a person may be convicted of a criminal offense in the absence of *mens rea.* This is called a strict liability offense. The two most common categories of strict liability offenses are (1) statutory rape—see discussion below and (2) a regulatory offense, where the goal of the criminal law is to regulate the social order rather than punish the offender (*e.g.* minor traffic offenses, food and drug laws).

C. NEGATIVE DEFENSES TO *MENS REA* (Failure of proof defenses)

A criminal actor may be able to raise a defense that some condition exists such that he does not have the requisite mental state for the crime. This is called a failure of proof defense because it operates to negate or negative the *mens rea* element.

1. **The defenses of intoxication.**

   a. **Voluntary Intoxication.** Modern common law takes the view that an actor, who is voluntarily intoxicated prior to the commission of a criminal act, may lack the mental capacity to form any state of mind higher than a general intent. Under this view, voluntary intoxication constitutes a partial defense, *i.e.,* a defense to a specific intent crime, but not to its general intent analog.

At a minimum, the actor, prior to imbibing to a state of drunkenness, is held to appreciate the uninhibiting influence of alcohol and the danger which a drunken actor portends for the world in general. In contrast, ancient common law perceived self-imbibing as an intentional pre-cursive step by a bad actor seeking the freedom of a more uninhibited state and therefore did not allow voluntary intoxication to be even a partial defense. This view continues to resonate with many juries.

MBE Advice

The MBE recently tested voluntary intoxication in the context of a theft offense. The actor in the question was on a bus and obviously intoxicated. While on the bus, he took a briefcase that he thought was his, but actually belonged to someone else. When the other party tried to retrieve his briefcase, the actor got in a fight and was charged with robbery. Because voluntary intoxication negated the specific intent to steal, the actor could not be convicted of robbery.

b. **Involuntary Intoxication.** Involuntary intoxication can operate as either a failure of proof defense, as in the case of voluntary intoxication by negating the *mens rea* of the crime (but both specific and general intent crimes are included), or as a complete defense under an excuse rubric (see outline below for discussion of excuse defenses). Involuntary intoxication can be a complete defense because it not only diminishes capacity the same as voluntary intoxication by virtue of the properties of the drug, but involuntary intoxication also exempts the defendant from general intent liability as well, since the involuntariness means the defendant never intentionally consumed a drug, and therefore there is no general intent to marry with the bad acts occurring while under the influence of the drug.

Common examples of involuntary intoxication include:

1) Innocent mistake

   Example: The defendant eats a brownie at a party without knowing that it contains hashish.

2) Trick

   Example: The defendant is offered a breath mint, but it actually is cocaine.

3) Duress

Example: Someone holds a gun to the defendant's head and demands that he ingest intoxicating liquor.

4) Medical advice, and

Example: The defendant is prescribed a medication that causes an unexpected intoxicating effect.

5) Pathological intoxication (grossly excessive reaction to intoxicant).

Example: The defendant's reaction is grossly excessive considering the amount of the intoxicant.

The resulting condition of the defendant must meet the jurisdiction's insanity test.

2. **Mistakes or ignorance.**
The basic rule is that ignorance or mistake of fact or law is a defense when it negates the existence of a mental state essential to the crime charged (thus a person cannot be convicted if she does not have the *mens rea* for the offense).

The basis for exculpation of an otherwise guilty actor, who acts pursuant to a mistake, is that a mistaken actor cannot avoid doing evil because he makes choices according to his mistaken perception, and not because he intended to do an evil act. However, mistakes are not necessarily an absolute or unqualified defense because the explanation behind making the mistake may still suggest a reckless disregard for others. Because different crimes require different levels of mental awareness or moral culpability, the validity of the mistake defense also turns on the level of mental awareness or culpability specified in the elemental definition of the crime and which the defense attempts to negate.

a. **Mistakes of fact.** At common law a mistake, or ignorance, of fact is a defense. The mistake must be honest (*i.e.*, subjective to the actor) to constitute a defense to a purpose or knowing (specific intent) crime. However, the mistake or ignorance of fact must be both honest and reasonable (*i.e.,* objective permissible as measured against a baseline of societal expectation) to constitute a defense to a reckless or negligent (general intent) crime.

Example: Suppose that D is being charged with the rape of A and claims he believed that A consented to the sexual intercourse. In fact, A did not consent. If a reasonable person would not have believed that A consented under the circumstances, D will be guilty of rape. In other words, D's good faith, but unreasonable mistake of fact as to consent will not be a defense to the general intent crime of rape.

Note: A mistake of fact is no defense if the fact as mistakenly believed would constitute no defense.

Example: Y stabbed A's brother, B. A followed Y with intent to stab Y. It was foggy and visibility was bad. A mistook X for Y and stabbed X. In this case, there was no right to stab either Y or X. Having a criminal intent and the act being *malum in se*, the mistaken identity is immaterial and gives A no defense.

b. **Mistakes of law.**

1) **Two kinds:** It is necessary to distinguish between two kinds of mistake of law:

a) **Defendant is unaware of the existence of a law making his conduct illegal.** In this first type, ignorance of the law is no excuse because everyone is presumed to know the law.

Example: A statute made it a criminal offense to vote in an election unless the voter had lived in the district for not less than 6 months. D, on the advice of a respected neighbor, voted at the election although he had not been in the district the required time. D honestly believed he had a right to vote. D is charged with violation of the statute. D's honest mistake or ignorance of the law is no defense. The offense is merely *malum prohibitum* and the only intent required by the statute is to do the prohibited act.

b) **Defendant makes a mistake concerning the legal effect of some collateral matter and that mistake results in his not understanding the full significance of his actions.** In this second type, a defense is available if the actor's mistake prevents her from forming the requisite intent.

Example: D was the owner of a large pile of corn on his farm. D owed C $100.00 which was long overdue. C honestly thought he had a right to collect the debt by helping himself to some of D's corn. He went to D's pile of corn and took exactly enough corn to equal the $100.00, according to the market. D was charged with larceny of the corn. D's honest belief that he had a right to take the corn in payment of the debt, a mistake of law, would negate any specific intent to steal, an essential element of that crime, and would be a good defense.

Note: The U.S. Supreme Court occasionally imposes a knowledge-of-illegality requirement upon *malum prohibitum* criminal statutes to ensure that the defendant acted with a wrongful purpose such as failure to report taxable income and where *malum prohibitum* nature of criminal statute did not provide notice to the defendant of the prohibited conduct because the duty imposed was less than obvious such as the imposition of a gun registration requirements.

2) **Two Other Types of Mistake of Law Defenses:** Mistake of law may operate in two other instances as an excuse defense (see outline below for discussion of excuse defenses).

a) Under the U.S. Supreme Court's opinion in *Lambert,* if the law punishes wholly passive conduct (such as failing to register as a felon) and the defendant was not put on notice of this requirement, then the actor may claim mistake of law as a defense.

b) If the actor can demonstrate reasonable reliance on an official pronouncement of the law that is later found to be in error, then the actor may have a valid mistake of law defense. Here, the actor must be able to point to an authoritative source for the law, such as the highest court in the jurisdiction. An attorney's advice will not suffice.

3. **Diminished capacity.**

The defense of diminished capacity is a partial defense available to those whose low IQ or limited mental capacity is said to preclude them from forming high levels of intent or deliberating at high levels of moral culpability. Compared to insanity, diminished capacity is understood as a lesser form of mental impairment.

a. **Common law.** The common law did not recognize the defense of diminished capacity. The rationale of this rejection is that at common law, once adjudged sane, all citizens were all on equal footing in their capacity and in their ability to distinguish right from wrong. The common law rationale made eminent sense in the simple world of common law crimes; it makes less sense in the more complicated world of regulatory crime and white collar crime.

b. **Modern statutes.** There is a split of statutory authority in this country as to acceptance of the diminished capacity defense. Those jurisdictions which accept the partial defense of diminished capacity recognize that evidence tending to negate specific intent is relevant to the existence of that intent. Thus, evidence of an abnormal mental condition not constituting legal insanity is competent for the purpose of negating a specific intent. Other jurisdictions adhere to the traditional approach, which takes such matters into account as sentencing factors.

4. **Entrapment.**

Entrapment is a controversial police undercover activity because even where judicially approved it frequently involves the government in the very same sleazy criminal activity it seeks to prosecute. The government must take care to trap the unwary criminal, not the unwary innocent.

a. **Definition.** Entrapment is the conception and planning of an offense by an officer, and his procurement of its commission by one who would not have perpetrated it except for the trickery, persuasion, or fraud of the officer. Although there are virtually unlimited entrapment scenarios, one excellent definition is that it is "an offer of the opportunity to commit an offense under controlled conditions."

A defendant who uses the defense of entrapment is admitting to committing the underlying offense. In short, a defendant who claims that he was entrapped by the Government must admit he committed the crime he was charged with. The elements of the defense are going to be determined by whether a jurisdiction uses the subjective view or the objective view.

1) **Subjective view.** The subjective view, which is the majority view, of the entrapment defense focuses on the question of criminal intent, *i.e.*, namely whether the defendant was predisposed to commit the crime. Under the subjective view, entrapment is a *mens rea* defense that must be evaluated by the trier of fact. The subjective entrapment defense has two elements:

a) **Was the offense induced by the government or a government agent?**

b) **Was the offender predisposed to commit the offense with which he was charged?** If the offender is predisposed to commit a crime, then the defense of entrapment is not available to the defendant. This prong allows the government to bring in all sorts of inadmissible evidence, such a prior offenses, to demonstrate an accused's predisposition to commit a crime.

2) **Objective view.** The objective view of entrapment focuses on the outrageousness of the government's role: "the conduct with which the defense of entrapment is concerned is the manufacturing of crime by law enforcement officials and their agents." Whether a particular defendant was "predisposed or otherwise innocent" is irrelevant, the important question is whether the Government's conduct in inducing the crime was beyond judicial tolerance. The objective view makes the evaluation of entrapment a matter of law concerning due process. It is, therefore, a defense to be evaluated by the trial judge. The objective approach has only one element, as defined in MPC 2.13: **Did the government agents cause a crime to be committed by employing methods of persuasion which create a substantial risk that such an offense will be committed by persons other than those ready to commit the crime charged?**

Example: Joe the tourist is visiting the ocean. Joe, who is a completely law-abiding individual, has never been convicted of any criminal offense. While visiting, Agent, working undercover, approaches Joe and offers him

$2 million dollars to carry a small quantity of cocaine back to his hometown. Joe repeatedly declines the offer, but after Agent finally offers Joe $3 million dollars, Joe reluctantly agrees. Joe is then arrested by Agent for trafficking in cocaine. Under both the subjective and objective defenses of entrapment, Joe would be acquitted of trafficking in cocaine.

D. CAUSATION

Causation is the third requirement for any result crime. *Mens rea, actus reus,* and causation are the three components for those crimes that require a particular result.

1. **Role of causation.** The role of causation is to connect the *actus*, or criminal act, to the *reus*, or criminal harm. Causation serves to ensure that to the extent possible, one criminal actor among many is singled out (personally responsible for the harm) and punished for exactly the level of moral culpability evidenced by his actions, no more, no less (reflecting the retributive and utilitarian goals of the imposition of the stigma of penal sanctions and of the goals of punishment).

   At common law, the concept of causation divided into two inquiries, **actual cause** or **"but for"** and **proximate causation** or **legal cause**. Both are required for criminal liability. "But for" cause defines the pool of persons whose actions are in a cause-in-fact relationship with the criminal harm, which has occurred. Proximate cause or legal cause operates to single out one definite cause-in-fact for recognition as *the* cause of concern to the criminal law.

2. **"But for" cause.** "But for" serves the limited purpose of excluding certain human acts that lack even a physical relationship to the resulting harm according to the laws of nature.

   a. **Physical conditions are not causes.** Thus, the first line of exclusion are conditions, *i.e.*, the physical laws of the universe, the interplay of inanimate objects and the like.

      Example: If A pushes B off of a building, it is the push by A, not the force of gravity, which goes into the pool of "but for" causers-in-fact.

   b. **Human acts having no bearing on a later event.** The second line of exclusion goes to acts which are not actual causes in fact in that they fall outside the chain of events.

      Example: Although A would not be available to push B off of a building, had A not been born, A's mother is excluded from the pool of but for causes because the act of giving birth to A is too far removed in terms of time, physical proximity, or logical connectedness to be contemplated as (objectively) reasonably foreseeable.

Prime fodder for testing foreseeability and culpability in causation. The classic criminal law problem, which brings principles of foreseeability and culpability to bear on causation, is the case of latent defects. The black letter rule at common law is that the criminal actor is held responsible for a victim's latent physical weakness, which makes the victim vulnerable beyond the intended consequences (you take the victim as you find her). However, the latent defects rule at common law is not absolute. There is no liability for unforeseen psychological quirks as a general rule. Likewise, results owing to latent defects, which go way beyond the kind of reasonable foreseeability or exceed the gravity of the intended consequence, are not held against the actor.

Example: If A slaps B intending moral instruction, but B has a fragile jaw which in fact is broken by the slap, A would be liable for breaking B's jaw. However, if A, during a prank, frightens B, but B has an arrhythmic heart condition or B has an extreme mental sensitivity to pranks, which is neither known by A nor reasonably foreseeable by him, A would likely escape liability for the unintended harm befalling B.

c. **Substantial Factor Test:**
In exceedingly rare circumstances, the "but for" test of actual causation is inadequate. Example: two criminals, A and B, inflict mortal wounds on the victim at exactly the same time. Neither can be said to be the "but for" cause. Would the victim have died but for A's act? Yes, B's act would have killed him, and vice versa. In this very rare circumstance, courts have adopted the "substantial factor" test for actual causation and asked if the criminal's action was a substantial factor in causing the death. Using the substantial factor test, both A and B are actual causes of the victim's death. Despite the seductive language of the "substantial factor" test, it should be used only in the rarest of cases.

3. **Proximate Cause.** The trick to properly conducting proximate causation analysis is the recognition that proximate cause is not discovered in a maze of common law rules or precedents, but rather is assigned on the basis of moral instinct of the analyzer. Causation exists in law as in science to tell us who or what, among various people or natural forces, is of interest. In criminal law our interest is in behavior modification and in moral condemnation. Thus, in criminal law, proximate cause exists to allow us to say who should be held morally responsible for a harmful result, *i.e.,* whose actions among a pool of "but for" causers are most in need of deterring. The purpose of the selection process is to focus corrective attention on blameworthy acts amenable to human control. The key factors in assessing proximate causation are: foreseeability and fairness.

Example: If A sets into motion a chain of events with the intention of harm befalling B, even though A relies on natural forces or other culpable actors, as the analyzer of the fact pattern you may appropriately single out A as the most culpable actor connected to B's harm and therefore argue that A is the proximate causer of the harm to B.

a. **Sequential cause.** Intervening forces can be dependent or independent. The common law rule is that an independent intervening force will supercede the moral culpability of the originating actor and break the chain of causation.

   Example 1: Assume A leaves a gun freely available to all who have access to his household. If A's minor son, thinking the gun is a toy, shoots A's other minor son with A's gun, A is liable for the shooting since his minor son's act of shooting was not borne of moral culpability and is therefore an intervening dependent force.

   Example 2: However, if during the commission of a burglary, the burglar shoots the same son with the same gun, A would escape liability for the shooting because the burglar's moral culpability in committing the felony is sufficient to supercede A's moral culpability in leaving the gun freely available. Therefore, the burglar's act is an independent intervening force.

b. **Concurrent causes.** Under common law if there are two equally culpable proximate causers for a single result, both are liable. This conclusion may be criticized as being intrinsically illogical because two people are punished for one result under a system designed to single out a single person for liability. But the alternative is less palatable: one goes free or worse, both go free. Although either cause would have resulted in harm, without either cause the harm would not have occurred precisely as it did.

   Example: If A kills B where B is already mortally wounded by another, A's secondary proximate cause arguably accelerated the result, while the originating proximate causer made B vulnerable to A's attack. Perhaps a better rationale is to say that since one purpose of criminal punishment is to deter bad actors, where there are two equally culpable bad actors, causation analysis correctly serves its intended function by identifying two bad actors who need deterring, even if (through no intent of their own) the results were limited to only one harmful result.

c. **Intervening Causes: Responses and Coincidences**
   Courts sometimes do not use the terminology of dependent or independent intervening causes and instead rely on the distinction between **responses** (reactions to the conditions created by the defendant) or **coincidences** (unrelated to the defendant's actions except that it places the victim at a particular time and place to be acted upon by the intervening cause). The general rule is that responses do not break the chain of causation unless they are abnormal and unforeseeable and that coincidences do break the chain of causation unless they are foreseeable.

Example: A shoots B. B is taken to the hospital and Dr. C gives him negligent treatment such that B dies. Dr. C's conduct is a response to A's act of shooting B. This response is neither abnormal nor unforeseeable (ordinary malpractice is said to be neither). Thus, the chain of causation is not broken and A is the proximate cause of B's death.

Example: A shoots B and leaves him in the roadway, where he is hit by a car driven by C. C hitting B with the car is a coincidence, but a foreseeable one. Thus, the chain of causation is not broken and A is the proximate cause of B's death.

II. COMMON LAW CRIMES INCLUDING MAJOR MISDEMEANORS

A. OFFENSES AGAINST THE PERSON

CRIMINAL HOMICIDE CHART

MURDER	MANSLAUGHTER
Malice Aforethought: 1) Intent to kill 2) Intent to cause grievous bodily injury 3) Depraved heart / extreme recklessness 4) Felony murder	*Voluntary: (intent to kill + mitigation)* 1) Heat of passion based on reasonable provocation 2) Imperfect self-defense 3) Diminished capacity
	Involuntary: 1) Recklessness or criminal negligence 2) Unlawful act – misdemeanor manslaughter

1. **Common Law: Criminal Homicide.** Common law homicide consists of the unlawful killing of a human being by another human being.

   Elements – common to all forms of criminal homicide:

   a. The **causal** (homicide is a result crime and the defendant must achieve the result of a dead body)

      Note on causation: Both actual and proximate causation must be proven.

   b. **killing** (*actus reus*) of

      Definition of death: Jurisdictions define death differently, *e.g.,* cessation of the heart, cessation of brain waves, *etc.*

The end of life: Although some jurisdiction may effectively authorize some form of euthanasia, mercy killings are not exempt from the prohibition against either homicide or suicide.

c. **Another, *i.e.,* a human being** (attendant circumstance that must be satisfied for liability to attach)

The beginning of life: At the common law, murder required that a child was born and was alive before it constituted a "human being" within the meaning of murder. Thus, the killing of a fetus did not constitute murder. Under the Supreme Court's decision in ***Roe v. Wade,*** it is permissible to exclude the consideration of a child in the womb as "another human being" and thus all jurisdictions exclude the killing of a child in the womb for medical reasons from homicide.

Non-medical killings of fetuses: An increasing number of jurisdictions authorize a homicide conviction for non-medical killing of a child in the womb. Such statutes also permit added punishment for battery of a pregnant woman who miscarries as a result.

2. **Murder** – Murder is the unlawful killing of a human being by another human being with malice aforethought. It consists of the following elements:

   a. *actus reus*—killing of

   b. another human being (attendant circumstance)

   c. *mens rea*—with malice aforethought

   d. actual and proximate causation—the criminal actor must achieve the result of a dead body

   a. **Malice Aforethought.** Malice aforethought is a catchall category consisting of four separate mental states, each of which is sufficient for the crime of murder. Malice aforethought also means that the defendant cannot claim a mitigating circumstance to reduce his crime to manslaughter (see below), or claim a complete excuse or justification defense.

      1) **A killing with the intention to cause death**,

      Example: A becomes angry at B because he does not like B's political views on a subject. A disagrees with B so much that he decides to kill him. One day, as B begins to expound on one of his dearly held views, A reaches into his pocket, pulls out a gun and shoots B. As such, this is a murder and A is guilty of the killing of A with malice aforethought.

2) **A killing with the intention to inflict grievous bodily injury to another,**

   Example: A becomes angry at B because he does not like B's political views on a subject. A decides that he is going to beat B "within an inch of his life" after one particularly energetic political exchange. A attacks B with a large club, striking B over the head multiple times. B is knocked unconscious and A continues to beat him. B lapses into a coma and dies the next day. A is guilty of murder even though he did not have the intent to kill because his actions constituted a killing with the intention to inflict grievous bodily injury on another. Under the common law, this type of killing constituted malice aforethought and met the mental state for murder.

3) **An extremely reckless disregard for the value of human life (the depraved heart murder),**

   Example: A loves explosions. He knows how dangerous they are, but still loves them nonetheless. Accordingly, A decides that seeing a petroleum tanker truck explode would be the greatest explosion he could imagine. A sees a full tanker truck, follows it, and then attaches a bomb to the side. The bomb goes off, igniting the tanker truck and causing it to explode. The ensuing explosion kills the tanker truck's driver and four innocent bystanders. A's actions, while lacking an intent to kill or an intent to do grievous bodily injury to another, are so reckless as to constitute a depraved heart killing because of the extremely reckless nature of his conduct. A's conduct, in this scenario, constitutes malice aforethought. The depraved heart murder requires the actor must subjectively understand the great risk his conduct creates even though he does not possess the intent to kill or the intent to do grievous bodily injury to another.

4) **An intention to commit a felony (the felony murder rule).**

   Example: A owns a dilapidated motel near the local airport. Needing money because of gambling debts, A decides to burn up the motel and use the insurance proceeds to pay off his gambling debts. A deliberately starts a fire in one of the rooms of the motel. The fire quickly spreads, burning down the entire motel. B, who was a resident of the motel, dies in the fire. A is guilty of murder because his actions during the commission of the felony of arson caused the death of B. This action constitutes malice aforethought and, consequently A is guilty of murder because of the felony murder rule.

b. **Proof of malice aforethought:** *Mens rea* is always proved by invoking the evidentiary tool known as an inference and is established by circumstantial evidence. Malice comes in two varieties: express and implied malice.

1) **Express malice:** A deliberate intention to unlawfully take away life of a fellow human being. It could mean:

   a) An actual intention to kill the person killed, or
   b) An actual intention to kill one person, but another is actually killed. (See also: doctrine of transferred intent).

2) **Implied malice:** Absence of either considerable provocation or attendant circumstances showing an abandoned and malignant heart. There is no actual intent to kill, but death is caused by an act, which discloses such an abandoned state of mind as to be equivalent to actual intent to kill.

   Murder occurs in three cases with implied malice:

   a) When the killing takes place with intent to cause grievous bodily injury,

   b) When the killing takes place under such circumstances which show a heart devoid of social duty and fatally bent on mischief (extreme recklessness), and

   c) When the killing takes place while in the commission of a felony.

   Note: There is no difference in legal effect between express and implied malice. If either is present, then the actor is guilty of murder.

   Example: A shoots into a crowd saying, "I hope I do not kill anyone," when the facts are such that the great and almost certain probability is that the act will kill someone. A is guilty of murder under a theory of extreme recklessness or depraved heart.

MBE Advice

MBE questions often focus on malice aforethought. Any killing with an extreme indifference to the value of human life will satisfy the requirements for a murder. When analyzing the MBE question, make sure that no "mitigating" factors exist that would lower the crime to a manslaughter.

3. **Felony murder rule.** The felony murder rule requires that the killing occur in attempting or committing the felony. Many commentators criticize the felony murder rule for the harsh result of permitting a murder conviction despite a felon's lack of culpability for the death or foreseeability of the fatal outcome.

There are four common limitations on the felony murder rule:

a. The felony must be **inherently dangerous** (Viewing the elements of the felony in the abstract, does this crime pose a significant risk to human life?)

b. The death must occur during the attempt or commission of, or immediately thereafter (Does the felony have a **time, place, and causal connection** to the death?)

c. The felony must be independent or have an **independent felonious purpose** (Generally, this excludes manslaughter, assault, and battery. No bootstrapping is allowed.)

d. **The felon must have done the killing** (Thus, a killing done by a police officer, bystander, or victim would be excluded from application of the rule. Focus on the killer not the victim.)

4. **Murder by Degree--Statutory Murder**. The common law did not distinguish murder by degrees. The degree distinction owes solely to statutory law and is important solely for punishment purposes.

DEGREES OF MURDER

First Degree:
1) Intent to kill with premeditation and deliberation. Look for poison, torture, bomb, or lying in wait on the MBE. Anything that indicates a plan or scheme to deliberately kill another is a good indication of premeditation and deliberation.
2) Felony murder with BARRK crimes (burglary, arson, rape, robbery, kidnapping).

Second Degree:
1) Intent to kill without premeditation and deliberation
2) Intent to cause grievous bodily injury
3) Depraved heart/extreme recklessness
4) Felony murder without BARRK crimes

a. **First degree murder** is that which is the result of "deliberation and premeditation," and felony murder during the commission of these specific felonies: BARRK (burglary, arson, rape, robbery, kidnapping).

b. **Second degree murder** is that which includes malice aforethought, but is not the result of "deliberation and premeditation," as well as the three other categories listed above.

c. The killing of one human being by another is presumed murder and the burden is on the accused to show:

1) Provocation reducing it to manslaughter, or

2) Excuse or justification.

d. In jurisdictions which divide murder into degrees, a first degree murder conviction enables the government to argue for the death penalty or life imprisonment without parole. Lesser degrees of murder limit the sentence to a term of years with a possibility for parole. Proof of first degree murder requires:

1) All elements of common law murder **plus**

2) **Deliberation:** A cool mind that is capable of reflection. Deliberation is sometimes thought of as weighing the pros and cons.

3) **Premeditation:** The cool mind did in fact reflect, at least for a short period of time before his act of killing. Premeditation is sometimes described as thinking about beforehand; or

4) **Felony Murder:** A killing which occurs during the commission or attempted commission of an inherently dangerous felony (BARRK crimes).

5. **Voluntary Manslaughter.** Voluntary manslaughter is the unlawful killing of a human being by another human being without malice aforethought. Voluntary manslaughter was a general intent felony at common law. Voluntary manslaughter is a killing that would be murder but for the existence of the mitigation, such as adequate provocation.

a. **Elements:** (criminal homicide without malice)

1) *actus reus*—killing of

2) another human being (attendant circumstance)

3) *mens rea*—without malice aforethought

4) actual and proximate causation

5) mitigating circumstances

b. **The *mens rea* of voluntary manslaughter.** The sole distinction between murder and voluntary manslaughter is the absence of malice aforethought--the *mens rea* of murder. Thus, voluntary manslaughter is a catch-all crime for

intentional homicide not amounting to murder. Adequate provocation such as disqualify intentional homicides as murder is defined as follows:

1) The most common mitigating circumstance that reduces murder to voluntary manslaughter is **heat of passion on reasonable provocation**.

   The elements of the heat of passion defense are:

   a) There must have been **reasonable provocation,**

   b) The defendant must have in fact been provoked,

   c) A reasonable man so provoked would not have cooled off in the interval of time between the provocation and the delivery of the fatal blow, and

   d) The defendant must not in fact have cooled off during the interval.

      Note: At common law, heat of passion was based on an immediate reaction. Under the MPC, heat of passion is expressed as extreme emotional disturbance to encompass the situation where the emotional response follows a prolonged festering.

2) **Adequate provocation.** Some of the situations in which the provocation has been held sufficient to reduce the intentional killing from murder to manslaughter include:

   a) Where the actor has been violently assaulted by the deceased.

   b) Where there has been an attempt to arrest the accused unlawfully.

   c) Where there has been mutual combat unsought by the accused, and

   d) Where one spouse sees the other spouse committing adultery and kills either adulterer.

   Example: A comes home to find his wife in bed with B, his business partner. A immediately attacks B and beats him to death. Under the common law, this provocation would be such that it mitigates A's conduct and removes the malice aforethought that would normally be necessary for such a killing. As such, this provocation does not excuse the killing completely, but does lower it to a voluntary manslaughter. On the MBE, do not analyze the question in order to find the crime of manslaughter. Instead, analyze the question for the crime of murder and see if it has any mitigation that would remove the *mens rea* of malice aforethought.

3) **Inadequate provocation.** Key to the *mens rea* of voluntary manslaughter is inadequate provocation which is provocation that is inadequate to completely justify the killing and exonerate the actor, but significant enough to have bearing on the wrongful act.

Examples of inadequate provocation would include a jealous husband or a miffed business partner.

Note on the reasonable person standard: Under a subjective standard, the provocation can be construed more favorably to the defense. In addition, the subjective standard would allow for more leeway in accessing each element of the heat of passion defense.

Watch Out!

Mere words alone without more, even the most insulting words, are never sufficient provocation to reduce murder to manslaughter. Even words with insulting gestures will not reduce a murder to manslaughter.

Example: X called D a son-of-a-bitch; whereupon D killed X. D is guilty of murder.

Watch Out!

Simple trespass alone either on land or on chattels is not sufficient provocation to reduce murder to manslaughter

c. **Manslaughter and Murder Distinguished**: Voluntary manslaughter differs from murder in that the killing is without malice. It differs from involuntary manslaughter in that it is done intentionally.

MBE Advice

Not only must there be provocation, but the killing must take place **in the heat of passion.** If the killing takes place after there has been time for the passion of a reasonable person to cool, then it is murder and not manslaughter.

On the MBE, look for the existence of a cooling off period or a short period in which the actor reflects before committing the killing. If the actor cooled off at any time during the chain of events, the crime is murder.

1) **Imperfect Self-Defense.** Another category of mitigation that reduces murder to voluntary manslaughter is **imperfect self-defense**. The key to imperfect self-defense is the premise that the perfect self-defense claim is not available to the actor because of the unreasonableness of his beliefs. For example, the actor may have believed that his life was in danger when a reasonable person would not. Accordingly, he would not be entitled to the self-defense exoneration from any criminal responsibility, but he may be entitled to an imperfect self-defense defense that could lower the crime from murder to manslaughter.

   Here, the criminal actor's self-defense claim is flawed for one of the following reasons:

   a) He used excessive force
   b) He was the initial aggressor
   c) His belief that death or serious bodily injury was imminent was not reasonable

2) **Diminished Capacity.** Finally, in some jurisdictions, **diminished capacity** mitigates murder to manslaughter.

6. **Involuntary Manslaughter.** Involuntary manslaughter is the **unintentional** killing of a human being by another human being by either (a) recklessness or criminal negligence or (b) in the commission of a misdemeanor. Involuntary manslaughter was a general intent felony at common law.

   Elements of Involuntary Manslaughter:

   a. *actus reus*—killing of

   b. another human being (attendant circumstance)

   c. *mens rea*—recklessness or criminal negligence (or in the commission of a misdemeanor)

   d. actual and proximate causation

   e1. **During reckless or criminally negligent performance of a lawful act.**

   Examples of a reckless death during a lawful act are a hunting accident or vehicular homicide:

   Example: D drives his automobile on the wrong side of the highway at night without lights which causes the death of W. D is guilty of involuntary manslaughter.

Involuntary manslaughter may also be committed by **omission to act when there is a duty to act.**

Example: H and W, husband and wife, go to a tavern and get drunk. Their house is only three blocks from the tavern. They walk home arm in arm when there is much snow on the ground and the temperature is below zero. When they are within a few feet of their house, the wife slips and falls in a snowdrift. H leaves W there and enters the house alone. The wife freezes to death. H owes a duty to rescue his wife but fails in the duty. H is guilty of involuntary manslaughter.

or

e2. **During the execution of an unlawful act**: This version of involuntary manslaughter is the misdemeanor-manslaughter rule, which operates like the felony murder rule. In general, the same types of limiters in terms of foreseeability, which constrict the felony-murder rule, apply here as well. The majority rule is to limit the misdemeanors qualifying for application of the rule to *malum in se* (inherently evil) misdemeanors and not *malum prohibitum* (prohibited by legislation) misdemeanors.

Examples of misdemeanor-manslaughter include death by fraternity hazing, drag racing, and Russian roulette.

Example: D was charged with the death of his two daughters. Although D did not affirmatively harm them in any way, he was guilty of the misdemeanor of willfully neglecting them. The neglect consisted in failing to protect them from the cruel physical abuses which were inflicted upon them by their mother, with D's knowledge, over a period of time, from which they died. D's conviction of manslaughter was sustained on the doctrine of misdemeanor-manslaughter.

7. **Mayhem or maiming.** Under the common law, the **felony** of mayhem is maliciously depriving another person of the use of such of his members (by dismemberment or disablement) as to render him less able, in fighting to defend himself or to annoy his adversary. The common law rationale for this crime was that the king would always have a healthy populace and be able to conscript soldiers. Modern statutes retain this offense, but no longer restrict it to injuries affecting the victim's ability to defend himself, and include permanent disfigurement.

   Elements of mayhem or maiming:

   a. *actus reus*: the act of maiming or disfiguring

   b. *mens rea*: maliciously or with specific intent to maim or disfigure

c. resulting in permanent dismemberment, disablement, or disfigurement, such as losing a hand, an eye, or castration

8. **Battery.** Battery was a general intent misdemeanor at common law. Battery is an unlawful application of force to the person of another, resulting in bodily injury or an offensive touching of one's body. Battery is a result crime, which means that causation must be shown.

   a. **Elements:**

      1) *actus reus*—unlawful application of force

      2) to the person (body) of another—attendant circumstance

      3) resulting in or causing bodily injury or offensive touching—causation required

      4) *mens rea*—intentionally, recklessly, or criminally negligently

      Note: Battery is a general intent crime. The element of an "intentional", reckless, or negligent application of force or touching is to rule out a purely accidental or unknowing touching (bumping someone in the elevator) or application of force (unintentionally startling an unsuspecting person).

   b. **Defenses.** Consent can be a defense to a simple battery. For example, boxing is a sport where the parties spend ten rounds inflicting batteries on each other.

   c. **Aggravated batteries.** Batteries committed with greater force, causing greater injury, or against certain kinds of victims are aggravated batteries or felonies, permitting greater punishment than that permitted for simple batteries. The rationale for the greater punishment is that aggravated batteries involve a greater social harm than does a simple battery. Thus, aggravated batteries include:

      1) Battery committed with a deadly weapon.

      2) Battery resulting in serious injury (requiring extensive medical attention).

      3) Battery against the president, police officers in the execution of their duties, pregnant women, and children are traditional aggravating factors. Recent legislation has focused on heightened punishment for violence against women and hate crimes.

   Example: At the local bar, A picks a fight with B. A throws the first punch and hits B in the face. B receives a black eye that can be readily treated with an icepack. A's first punch was a battery. However, A does not stop. He punches B again, breaking his nose and splitting his lip in a manner that will require stitches. A has now committed an aggravated battery. If A had used a deadly weapon to commit the injuries or B was a member of a protected class, those crimes would also constitute aggravated batteries. When examining these problems, look to whether the victim is a member of a specific, protected class and/or the seriousness of the victim's injuries to see if the battery is enhanced to an aggravated battery.

9. **Assault.** Assault was a specific intent misdemeanor at common law.

   Caution #1: Practitioners commonly refer to batteries and assaults alike as assaults. However, the bar exam tests your understanding of the formal distinction between assault and battery.

   Caution #2: There were two different forms of assault recognized at common law. Analyze exam problems under both forms.

   a. **Assault Form #1 – Attempted-battery assault.** The first form of assault sees the offense as an attempted battery (or more realistically, a battery that failed). This view of battery focuses on the mind of the assailant—what was the intent—rather than that of the harm to the victim.

      Assault Form #1—Attempted-battery assault
      Elements:

      1) *actus reus*—threatening conduct (essentially an attempt to batter)

      2) *mens rea*—intent to batter (or injure)

      3) present ability—proximity analysis

      Defenses: Under Form #1, the assault requires "present ability," since ability bears on the intent of the assaulter. Thus, under Form #1, pointing an unloaded gun at one would not be an assault—this would be an attempt of an assault. This is the minority rule. (See anticipatory offenses below).

   b. **Assault Form #2 – Intentional-scaring assault.** Unlawfully submitting one to the apprehension of force or the person of another, *i.e.*, an offensive touching of one's mind.

      Assault Form #2—Intentional scaring assault
      Elements:

      1) *actus reus*—threatening conduct (conduct that scares)

2) *mens rea*—intent to scare or frighten the victim
3) creation of a reasonable apprehension of an immediate physical harm (essentially a battery)

Defenses: Form #2 assault focuses on the effect on the victims' state of mind. Under Form #2, "present ability" is irrelevant. Thus, pointing a gun at someone who did not know the gun was not loaded would constitute an assault because it places another in reasonable apprehension of immediate physical harm. Thus, under assault form #2, reasonable apprehension makes the lack of intent or ability to do a battery unimportant. This is the majority rule.

Example Assault Form #1: Driving home from work, A is cut off by B. At a stoplight, A gets out of his car, runs up to B's driver side window and begins to threaten him. A is really angry and wants to hurt B because of his crazed driving manner. A bangs on B's driver's side car window and B begins to giggle. A becomes even angrier and attempts to open the car door to get at B. B, laughing because of A's maddened condition, locks his doors and drives off before A can cause him any injury. In this scenario, this is an Assault Form #1 because the primary focus is on A's intent, not the result of his actions. B thought it was funny, but A was engaging in this conduct in order to injure B. Despite the fact that no injury occurred, this was an Assault Form # 1 crime.

Example Assault Form #2: Driving home from work, A is cut off by B. At a stoplight, A gets out of his car, runs up to B's driver side window and begins to threaten him. A does not really want to hurt B, but does want to teach him a lesson. A tells B that he is going to kill him and dares him to get out of the car. A paces around the car, banging on the B's driver's side window and threatening B. B is so frightened that he calls the police on his cell phone and speeds off when A is not in front of his car. As such, this is an Assault Form #2 because of the effect on the victim. The actor's conduct, coupled with the victim's state of mind is the key to the analysis.

B. OFFENSES AGAINST SEXUAL AUTONOMY

1. **Rape**. Rape was a general intent felony at common law. The elements of rape are as follows:

   a. **Elements:**

      1) sexual intercourse (vaginal penetration)

      Carnal Knowledge. At common law, rape required carnal knowledge of a woman. Carnal knowledge essentially means vaginal penetration. It is an essential element of the crime that the male insert his sex organ into the female sex organ. Emission is not required.

2) with a woman, not the defendant's wife (the marital exemption)

Committed by men against women. At common law, rape could only be committed by men against women. If the act of rape was committed against a man, the charge was sodomy.

Marital status. The parties cannot be married. This is sometimes referred to as the marital exemption to rape.

3) by force or threat of force

Force Requirement. The sexual penetration must occur by either actual physical force (e.g., beating the victim), a verbal threat of serious bodily injury (e.g., "I will kill you unless you comply."), or the brandishing of a weapon (e.g., a gun or knife).

Example: A is walking home from work one evening. She takes a short cut through a dark alley. B, whom A does not know, approaches A. B tells her that he will stab her if she does not take of her clothes and submit to being raped. A takes off her clothes and B rapes her. B is guilty of rape because the threat of bodily injury will satisfy the requirement of force.

4) without her consent (or against her will)

Lack of Consent. A lack of consent can be established by in a variety of ways. The use of actual force, threat, or weapon helps to verify non-consent on the part of the woman. A lack of consent can also be established where the woman lacks capacity to consent due to such factors as unconsciousness or sleep, mental illness or condition, intoxication, or age (see below for statutory rape). In these cases, the law presumes non-consent.

Example: A drinks way too much and becomes intoxicated at the company holiday party. B, her male secretary, agrees to drive his boss home. In the car, A passes out and B undresses her and has sexual intercourse with her. B is guilty of rape because A could not consent due to her intoxicated state.

The Effect of Fraud on Consent. On one hand, fraud in the factum (a mistake about whether the victim is engaging in an act of sexual intercourse) vitiates consent. For instance, it would be fraud in the factum if a doctor pretended to perform a medical procedure, but engaged in sexual intercourse with the victim. On the other hand, fraud in the inducement does not prevent effective consent because the woman knows that she is consenting to an act of sexual intercourse and is only misled as to the reasons (or inducements) for doing so. For example, if the defendant pretended to be a star athlete and thus obtained the victim's consent, no rape would have occurred.

Example: A tells B, an attractive woman in her early 20s, that he is the executive producer of a reality TV show. B, who has aspirations of becoming an actress, accompanies A back to his hotel room. While in the room, A has consensual sex with B. The next morning, B discovers that A is a mailman in reality. B feels that she A misled her and goes to the police. A is not guilty of rape. A may have lied to B about his true profession, but the sexual intercourse was consensual. Accordingly, no crime has been committed.

b. **Note on the *mens rea* of rape.** The *mens rea* of rape is implied by the mistake of fact defense. Rape is a general intent crime. Defenses going to negate knowledge of a lack of consent, such as mistake of fact on the question of consent or voluntary intoxication on the part of the defendant, constitute a partial defense. The effect of the partial defense is to permit an instruction on a lesser included offense such as sexual assault. American jurisdictions tend to require a good faith and reasonable mistake regarding consent.

c. **Statutory reform.** Modern statutes have eliminated or significantly altered the common law elements of rape.

1) Marital rape exception is either eliminated or restricted to situations where the parties are not estranged and where there is no physical violence.

2) Most jurisdictions expand the concept of rape to include male and child victims. The common law crime of sodomy and many offenses against children have been merged into rape.

3) Rape can apply to unlawful sexual penetration of various human apertures and oral sex. Further, in many cases, rape is not limited to using the male sex organ. Any part of the human anatomy, or any inanimate object, inserted into vaginal or anal cavity of another constitutes rape.

d. Date rape is prosecuted on a theory of overbearing aggression by the man versus critical analysis of the consent by the woman.

2. **Statutory Rape.** Statutory rape usually includes all the elements above, and in addition thereto specifically requires that the female is legally incompetent to give consent if she is under a certain age, such as eighteen. The crime of "carnal knowledge of a child" is unlawful intercourse with a willing female child who is under the age of consent. Such conduct is made a crime, usually a felony, by

statute, and although not so named by statute is commonly known as "statutory rape."

Example: A, a college student, is at a cook-out. While at the cook-out, A met a strikingly beautiful female named B. B was drinking a beer. A noticed that B is six feet tall and wearing her hair and make-up in a very mature manner. When speaking with B, A noticed that she is well read and very intelligent. B tells A that she is a freshman at the local university. A talks to B the entire evening and takes her back to his apartment. A and B engage in consensual sex. The next morning B leaves. Two days later, the police arrive and arrest A. A discovers that B, despite all the reasonable indications to the contrary, was a 12 year old girl. A is guilty of statutory rape.

MBE Advice

On the MBE, "mistake as to age is not a defense to statutory rape" will be your best answer choice, since statutory rape is a strict liability crime.

3. **Sodomy**. Sodomy was a common law felony. The common law elements of sodomy were anal intercourse or *per os* between men or animals. Most jurisdictions require an additional element of force as a prelude to prosecution.

C. OFFENSES AGAINST FREE MOVEMENT

1. **Kidnapping**. Kidnapping was a general intent misdemeanor at common law. The elements of kidnapping at common law are as follows.

   a. **Forcible taking and**

   b. **Carrying away (asportation)**

   c. Of **another**

   d. **To another country**.

   Example: A grabs his ex-wife B when she is on her way to work. He forces her into a car, ties her up, and then drives her to Mexico. While in the car, B begs A to let her go and tells him that she will never love him. A ignores her pleas as he is determined that she will love him if they can begin anew in Mexico. Once the car crosses into Mexico, A releases his ex-wife. A is guilty of kidnapping.

2. **Modern kidnapping**. Following the alleged kidnapping-death of the Lindbergh baby in the 1930s, American jurisdictions elevated kidnapping to heinous or most serious felony status. The statutory revision goes to the effect on the victim.

   a. **Elements:**

      1) The unlawful and intentional taking (seizing, confinement) **of another by**

      2a) **Asportation** (movement of any sort is sufficient)

      or

      2b) **Confinement, including mere detention, if done with the requisite intent to conceal the person in a secret place**

   b. **Aggravated kidnapping elements:**

      1) **Movement or detention for the purpose of**

      2) **Infliction of bodily harm**

      or **obtaining of money or property**

      or **commission of any sexual offense**

      or **child stealing**

   c. **Defenses:** Lack of capacity vitiates consent as an affirmative defense to kidnapping. Thus, children, victims of felonies (other than the kidnapping), the intoxicated, and the insane lack the capacity to consent to the kidnapping.

3. **False imprisonment.** False imprisonment, a general intent misdemeanor at common law, is the unlawful confinement of a person. Essentially, it involves the use of force or threat of force to cause a person to stay where they are do not wish to stay or go where they do not wish to go. False imprisonment is a lesser included offense in the charge of kidnapping.

   a. **Elements:**

      1) **unlawful** (e.g., not authorized by law, without consent)

      2) confinement or detention of a person

   b. **Defenses.** Merely blocking a doorway is not false imprisonment so long as other escape routes are available.

D. OFFENSES AGAINST PROPERTY INTERESTS (THEFT OFFENSES)

THEFT OFFENSES – OVERVIEW

LARCENY –	trespassory taking and carrying away of the personal property of another with intent to steal
ROBBERY –	larceny plus (1) force or fear and (2) person or presence
EMBEZZLEMENT –	stealing by one with lawful possession of the property based on a trust relationship
FALSE PRETENSES –	acquiring **title** to the property by the stealing

1. **Larceny**. Larceny was a specific intent felony at common law. Larceny was the only common law theft offense. The common law elements of larceny are as follows.

   a. The **taking** (caption):

      Note: A taking occurs when the Actor exercises control either directly or indirectly by using a third party. Dominion and control means an act inconsistent with rights of superior property interest.

   b. By **trespass** and (without consent): against the possessory interests of another

      Watch Out!

      The concept of **"trespass"** of personal property in the law of larceny is different from the use of that term as it relates to real property – as in "he trespassed on my land."

   c. **Carrying away** (asportation): some movement however slight
      There must be an exercise of complete dominion over the personal property, even if only for an instant and if transported through only a millimeter of space.

      Example: A, a pickpocket, reached into B's coat pocket and took hold of B's wallet and lifted it two inches from the bottom of the pocket when B grabbed his wallet. There was an asportation.

Example: A goes into the hills and discovers B's grazing cow. He shoots the cow, skins the hind quarters and drags them under a tree. In a charge against A for larceny of the cow, transporting any part of the carcass of the cow any distance constitutes asportation.

Example: A grabbed a raincoat which was chained to a dummy in front of B's store. He started to run with the coat but the chain held it and A was scared away. There was no asportation because A never had dominion of the coat.

d. Of the **tangible, personal property**

Note on the *res* of common law larceny. Common law larceny limited the crime to taking of tangible, personal property of another. Modern statutes expand the crime to takings of services and other intangible property. Real estate cannot be the *res* of larceny. However, if crops are severed from the land, for instance, and subsequently stolen, then they may be subject to larceny.

Note: Anything not real property which has value of the minutest degree or has become a subject of barter and sale in the stream of commerce may be personal property and the subject matter of larceny, even though it was not such at the early common law.

Example: Dogs and cats, not the subject of larceny in the early law, are now considered subjects of barter and sale. Also, captured wild animals, impounded water, gas, and electricity held for commercial purposes.

e. Of **another** (the *actus reus*)

Watch Out!

One cannot steal from one's self. This applies to instances of joint ownership as well.

f. With **intent to steal** (*i.e.*, **permanently** deprive; the *mens rea*).
Note on deprivation versus taking in larceny. Note that the intent to steal can be established either on a theory of taking (*i.e.*, the Actor intends to acquire the property of another) or on a theory of depriving (*i.e.*, the Actor intends that the owner no longer have his property).

2. **Wrongful appropriation.** Where the intent is only to **temporarily** borrow, the crime is wrongful appropriation, a lesser included offense to larceny.

3. **Conversion.** Larceny requires the formation of intent to steal to occur simultaneously with the taking. If the Actor takes possession at one point in time and later decides to steal the property, the crime is conversion, not larceny. In other words, the *mens rea* and *actus reus* must coincide.

   a. **Delivery by mistake.** Mistakes are generally exam fodder to test knowledge of the larceny/conversion dichotomy. If the initial receipt of the chattel is innocent, its subsequent conversion cannot be larceny, because the felonious intent does not coincide with the taking. But, if the recipient knows at the time he is receiving more than his due and intends to convert it to his own use, he is guilty of larceny. This proposition can be restated as two separate rules.

   b. **Rule of unilateral mistake.** When a transferor acts under a unilateral mistake of fact, his delivery of a chattel may be ineffective to transfer title or his right to possession. If the transferee, knowing of the transferor's mistake, receives the goods with the intention of appropriating them, his receipt and removal of them is a trespass and his offense is larceny. However, for larceny to attain, the transferee must know of the mistake at the time of receipt. If he only learns of the mistake after acquiring possession, the offense is conversion.

   c. **Rule of mutual mistake.** However, if there is a mutual mistake because both the transferor and transferee have no knowledge of an exchange, then the law of lost and found applies and the transferee's actions with felonious intent upon discovery of the mistake would constitute larceny.

   d. **Lost and found property. The rule of lost goods:** If the finder, at the time of the finding, intends to deprive the owner permanently of his property, and if he knows or has a reasonable clue as to whom the owner is, he is guilty of larceny.

      1) Thus, the first testable issue in lost and found factual scenarios concerns the existence of identifiable ownership traits.

      2) The second issue concerns the occurrence of conduct inconsistent with that of the owner. This is so because knowledge of the owner's identity at the time of the taking in conjunction with conduct inconsistent with the owner's interest gives rise to a possible inference of the intent to steal. Care must be observed in constructing this inference since the finder is not duty bound to use diligence to search for the owner, and the finder's belief regarding the owner turns on the circumstances apparent to him at the time of finding the property.

      3) **Proof of subsequent intent.** Conversion may be shown either by direct proof of the fact of conversion, or, in the case of public officials, by proof of a demand and a refusal. Proof of conversion by a demand and refusal is

limited to embezzlement by public officials where the existence of a public trust implies an affirmative duty to respond to a demand.

4) Thus, no larceny exists if:

   a) the actor intends to keep the property but does not know who the owner is or have reason to believe that she can be identified

   b) the actor knows who the owner is but takes property with intent to return it and subsequently changes her mind

e. **Breaking the bulk doctrine.** Under the common law, bailees had lawful possession of property entrusted to their care. Thus, larceny could not occur with respect to bailments. The common law developed the breaking the bulk doctrine to deal with this problem. If a bailee stole the whole bale (or package), then it would not be larceny because the bailee was in lawful possession of the bale. However, if the bailee broke the bulk and stole part of the contents, then it could be larceny on the theory that the bailee did not have lawful possession of the contents of the bale.

4. **Larceny by Trick** – In the case of larceny by trick, the consent to the taking is fraudulently induced. Some courts speak of a constructive trespass. Other courts say that "fraud vitiates the transaction."

   The elements of larceny by trick are as follows:

   a. A **false representation** of a material present or past fact

   b. Which **causes** the victim

> **Watch Out!**
>
> The owner must have relied upon the actor's knowing misrepresentation.

   c. To **pass possession of**

   Note: When title is passed, the crime is "false pretenses," if only possession passes, the crime is "larceny by trick". These are mutually exclusive crimes.

   d. The **property** to the wrongdoer

   e. Who **knows the representation to be false** and

f. **Intends thereby to defraud the victim**.

Example: A borrows B's automobile for a short trip. A gives B his correct name but a false address. Later that day, A sells B's car to C and absconds with the proceeds from the sale. A is guilty of larceny by trick. The consent of B was fraudulently induced by A and constituted a constructive trespass to possession of the vehicle.

5. **False Pretenses** – The crime of obtaining property by false pretenses is statutory in origin. It is usually defined as: knowingly and designedly, and with intent to defraud, obtaining the property of another. This crime deals with the ***title and ownership* of property**, as distinguished from larceny by trick, which deals only with ***possession***.

The elements of obtaining property by false pretenses are as follows:

a. There must be a **representation of fact**, past or present.

b. The representation must be **false**.

c. The accused must **know that it is false**.

d. The accused must **intend to defraud**.

e. The owner of the property must **rely on the misrepresentation** and be defrauded, having a right to rely thereon.

f. The owner must **part with title to his or her property** in reliance on the misrepresentation.

Watch Out!

Promises to do something in the future, or mere statements of opinion, or mere seller's talk of "puffing" concerning the quality of the seller's wares, will not support a conviction for this crime.

Example: A is an unscrupulous real-estate hustler with felony criminal history. A tells B that she can buy into a huge real estate consortium for $100,000. A tells B that she will at least double her money and that there is no possible way for her not to make money. A tells B that this is her one chance to make money like those Wall Street fat cats and to hurry up and join this consortium. B, who is 78 years old, lives alone on a fixed income salary.

She has nothing but her house and the money that comes from social security. B asks A if he will accept title to her house in order for her to buy into this real estate consortium. A agrees and B signs over the title to her house. A has committed the crime of False Pretenses.

6. **Embezzlement.** Embezzlement was not a crime at common law, but was made a crime by English statute. The elements of embezzlement are:

   a. The **fraudulent**

   b. **Conversion** of
   Conversion means to act on property in a manner seriously inconsistent with trust relationship underlying the owner's willing transfer of possession.

   c. The **tangible personal property of another**

   d. By one who is already in **lawful possession** of it

   e. By virtue of a **trust relationship**

   f. With **intent to steal/permanently deprive**

   Note on custody versus possession: Embezzlement turns on the Actor's misuse of a position of trust to acquire the property of another. Low-level employees such as the cleaners lack such a high position and thus their taking a sip of liquor from the liquor closet would constitute larceny because they had custody not possession. In contrast, the butler or executive secretary occupies a position of trust and is deemed to have possession of property on behalf of the principal and thus their sipping the liquor would breach their trust relationship and constitute embezzlement.

   Example: A is a stockbroker. A manages B's equities account that consists of a number of "blue chip" stocks. The stocks are registered in B's named but are managed by A. A has been B's family stockbroker for years. A also has a gambling addiction. A sells B's stocks and gives the proceeds to his bookie. A is guilty of embezzlement.

   Note: The four theft crimes (larceny, larceny by trick, false pretense, and embezzlement) are all specific intent crimes.

7. **Forgery.** Forgery was a general intent misdemeanor at common law. The elements at common law follow:

   a. ***Actus reus*:** Material false making or alteration of a writing or document of some legal significance.

MBE Advice

Forgery at common law required the forged document to be of legal significance. Recent MBE questions have tested this concept by presenting a set of circumstances that would suggest a forgery, but for the lack of a legally significant document.

b. ***Mens rea*:** with intent to defraud.

8. **Receipt of stolen goods.** Receipt of stolen goods is a statutory offense whose common law origin, if any is not clear. The elements at common law of receipt of stolen goods follow.

   a. ***Actus reus*:** taking possession of stolen property

   b. ***Mens rea*:** with knowledge that it has been stolen (*i.e.,* acquired in a manner constituting larceny or theft) and with intent to deprive the owner of it.

   The receipt of the property means merely that there shall be such exercise of dominion over the property that it is made more difficult for it to be located by the law enforcement agencies.

   Example: A's brother, B, stole a gold brick and covered it with cloth making it appear as a door stop and placed it by the front door in A's house. The police came to A's house. When A opened the door to admit them he kicked the gold brick door stop behind the door with his foot, which made it more difficult to be found. A's act constituted a receiving.

   Subjective Test: The property must have been stolen in fact. It is not enough that it has been embezzled or obtained by false pretense or converted to one's use through the commission of a tort.

   The accused must know it was stolen property when he receives it. This does not mean actual knowledge but means merely that the accused believed it was stolen or that he had a faint suspicion that it was stolen. The test is subjective, and refers to the defendant personally, and not objective, referring to the defendant as a reasonable person.

   Wrongful Intent: There must be wrongful intent. This means the purpose of the receipt must be other than innocent or with *mens rea.* For one to receive known stolen property for the purpose of returning it to the rightful owner or to detect the thief would negate the existence of the crime. Mere naked possession of property which has recently been stolen is not sufficient to prove guilty knowledge.

Example: D was convicted of receiving stolen property. The evidence showed that stolen apparel was found in D's store, both in his vault and on open racks. D contended that he purchased the goods from a jobber. In reversing a conviction, the court held that mere possession did not establish guilt beyond a reasonable doubt. There must be guilty knowledge.

9. **Malicious mischief.** Malicious mischief is a general intent statutory offense. The **elements** of the offense are as follows:

   a. **Malicious destruction of the property**

   b. **Of another.**

E. OFFENSES AGAINST PERSONS AND PROPERTY

1. **Robbery.** Robbery was a common law felony. Robbery is essentially larceny plus battery (force) or assault (fear). It is a specific intent crime.

   a. The elements of robbery at common law are as follows:

      1) All six elements of **Larceny**, plus two additional elements:

      2) The property is taken from the victim's **person** (physical body) or from the victim's **presence** (presence means that the property must be with the proximity and control of the victim so that he or she can feel the results of the force element. If the object is so far away that the victim cannot be intimidated by the force then it is not within the presence of the victim.); and

      3) The taking is accomplished by means of **force** or the **threat of imminent force**.

      Key to robbery: Robbery is a dual offense in that it is an offense against both the security interests of people and property.

MBE Advice

Recent MBE fact patterns have described a crime that looked like robbery except that the crime in question was missing one of the essential elements of larceny. Given such a fact pattern, **robbery** would be a wrong answer choice.

Remember, in order to have a robbery, all the essential elements of larceny must be satisfied.

b. **Aggravated Robbery**. Aggravated Robbery was created by statute and requires a robbery with use of a deadly weapon or the infliction of serious bodily harm.

2. **Extortion at common law.** Extortion is a crime against the administration of justice or the conduct of the government. Extortion was a general intent misdemeanor at common law. The common law definition was:

   a. **Collection** by an official **of a fee**

   b. **under color of office**

   c. **without authority** (corruptly)

MBE Advice

The key to the *common law* offense was related to the administration of justice or performance of official government duties. Recent MBE trends have created a crime similar to extortion, but lacking the governmental aspect of the crime. Without that element, the crime is not extortion *at common law.*

3. **Extortion under modern statutes.** The modern statutory revision of extortion expanded the crime to include a gravamen against interests in property. The modern statutory elements of extortion are as follows:

   a. **Larceny**

   b. Taking where the intimidation is **a threat of future harm** to the possessor or someone in her company

4. **Blackmail.** Blackmail is a lesser offense to extortion. The offense is essentially making a threat to obtain property. The offense of blackmail describes offenses in which the threats of future harm are less than threats to do bodily harm. Such lesser threats include threats to damage property, to accuse the victim of a crime, or to reveal certain types of information concerning the victim.

   Example of Common Law Extortion: A is a policeman. A stops B for speeding. A tells B he will let him go for a small fee. A gives B $50.00 and pulls off. Because A has used his office to collect a fee he is not entitled to, he has committed the crime of extortion.

Example of Statutory Extortion: A loves B's baseball card collection. A likes B's collection so much that he approaches B and tells him that he will shoot B tomorrow if he does not give A the baseball card collection. Statutory extortion was designed to fill in the gap when certain crimes were more than larceny, but not quite robbery because of a lack of immediate force.

Example of Blackmail: A loves B's baseball card collection. A likes B's collection so much that he approaches B and tells him that he will burn B's car if he does not give A the baseball card collection. The threats are less than that of bodily harm and, as a result, the crime is blackmail, not extortion.

F. OFFENSES AGAINST THE SECURITY OF HABITATION INCLUDING PERSONS AND PROPERTY

1. **Burglary.** Burglary was a specific intent felony at common law. It was a crime against the habitation rather than the property. It protected people in their homes from criminal offenses. The common law elements of burglary are as follows:

   a. The **breaking**, and

   Note: Breaking (at common law) served to indicate the strength of the actor's purpose. Contemporary law replaces the requirement of breaking with that of non-consensual entry.

   Watch Out!

   A breaking may be actual or constructive.

   An **actual** breaking is accomplished by the even the most minute moving of any part of the house such as pushing further open a door which is ajar, removal of a screen or window or opening an unlocked or locked door. The breaking must always precede the entry. If the breaking is after the entry, there is no burglary.

   A breaking is **constructive** when the entry is gained by trick, fraud, fear, or by conspiracy, such as opening a door from the inside by a confederate.

   Breaking has been held to include sliding down a chimney.

   b. **Entering** of

   Note: This means that there must be an entry into the dwelling house of at least some part of the body, such as a hand, head, or finger. The slightest entering is sufficient. Or the entry may be by an instrument, such as reaching through an opened window with a cane on the end of which is a piece of gum to pick up a diamond ring on a table. The instrument must be capable of effectuating the actor's criminal intent. Thus, throwing a baseball through a window is sufficient to satisfy breaking, but entry would still have to occur by use of the body or another instrument. Entry, even if immediately withdrawn, is sufficient.

c. The **dwelling** house

Note: The importance of the dwelling requirement has to do with the right to be safe in one's own home or castle. Contemporary law expands dwelling to go beyond residences to include buildings commonly associated with and in near proximity to the residences; some jurisdictions refer to any buildings within the curtilage as part of the dwelling house proper if used in connection therewith and in close proximity. Movable residences, such as house trailers, are properly classified as dwellings. Many burglary statutes also extend the dwelling place to include vehicles.

d. Of **another**

Note: The dwelling house must be that of another. This has reference to occupancy rather than ownership. A landlord may be guilty of burglarizing his own house if it is occupied by a tenant. The reason for this is that this crime is an aggression not against the property as such, but against the habitation of human beings and is intended to protect the occupants against the danger of entry by felons.

e. At **night**

Note: Night means between sunset and sunrise. Night requirement has been eliminated in contemporary law by statute.

MBE Advice

Recent MBE fact patterns have described a crime resembling burglary, but taking place during the daytime. If the crime does not occur at night, it cannot be considered burglary *at common law.*

f. With the **intent to commit a felony within**. (the *mens rea).*

Note: This means that the accused at the time of breaking and entering must have had the intent to commit a felony in the dwelling house. The intent to commit a felony which is subsequently formed (after the felon has broken and entered) is not sufficient. Any intent other than to commit a felony, regardless of its nature, is not sufficient. It is totally immaterial whether or not the intended felony is actually committed.

Example: A notices that B has a beautiful new big screen TV. A can see this TV through the picture window of B's house. One night, at midnight, A decides he is going to steal the TV. He breaks the lock on the door to B's house, goes inside, and takes the TV. A has committed a burglary.

Example: A notices that B has a beautiful new big screen TV. A can see this TV through the picture window of B's house. One night, at midnight, A decides he is going to look at the TV. He breaks the lock on the door to B's house, goes inside, and approaches the TV. Once A sees the TV up close, he likes it even more than before and decides to take it. A has not committed a burglary because the intent to steal was not formed until after he entered the home.

2. **Arson.** Arson was a general intent felony at common law. The common law elements of arson are as follows:

   a. **Willful, malicious, or wanton** (extreme recklessness): This means that the burning must be intentional, without justification or excuse. Any burning by accident or negligence, even gross, is not sufficient. However, wanton or extremely reckless conduct is enough. A specific intent to burn or destroy is not required.

   Example: If A unintentionally sets fire to B's house while committing a burglary therein, the burning is not willful and malicious and does not constitute arson. However, the deliberate burning of a dwelling house of another merely for the excitement of seeing a fire is a willful and malicious burning.

   b. **Burning** of: (Expanded to include other types of destruction by fire such as explosions).

   There must be a burning, which means that some of the substance of which the building is made must be burned. The slightest burning, such as a live cinder imbedding itself in a wooden shingle on the roof is sufficient. But merely scorching or causing discoloration is not sufficient.

   c. The **dwelling** (Expanded by statutes to any building and to vehicles).

   Any building regularly slept in is a dwelling house. Such is the test. The dwelling house includes the barn, smokehouse and other outbuildings within the curtilage used in connection therewith.

Example: A barn separated by a highway from the dwelling house proper is ***not*** part of the dwelling house.

d. Of **another.**

This has reference to occupancy rather than ownership. Hence, a landlord may be guilty of arson of a house which he owns, but which is occupied by his tenant.

G. ANTICIPATORY OFFENSES – SOLICITATION, CONSPIRACY AND ATTEMPT

It may be helpful to think of crimes as being arrayed along a continuum, from least to most complete: **solicitation ➔ conspiracy ➔ attempt ➔ offense**.

1. **Solicitation.** Solicitation (incitement) was a common law specific intent, misdemeanor crime.

   a. **Elements:**

      1) *Actus reus:* **Asks, incites, invites, requests, commands, or encourages** another to engage in conduct constituting any felony or a serious misdemeanor relating to obstruction of justice or a breach of the peace,

      2) *Mens rea:* With the **intent that the person commit the crime.**

   b. **Defenses:**

      1) It is no defense that the solicitant does not respond, is not convicted, or that it was factually impossible to complete the offense solicited under the circumstances. The solicitant need not even be aware of the solicitation.

         Key to solicitation. Regardless of whether the inducements prove successful, there is a concern to protect citizens from being exposed to inducements to commit or join in the commission of the crimes.

      2) The majority rule is that neither renunciation nor withdrawal is a defense. However, renunciation or successfully preventing the crime is an affirmative defense to solicitation under MPC § 5.02.

   c. **Merger.** Solicitation is essentially an attempted conspiracy; the moment the solicitant agrees to commit an offense, the solicitation merges into a conspiracy, an attempt to commit a crime, or the completed crime.

Example of Solicitation: A asks B to help him destroy evidence of A's illegal drug trafficking. B does not respond. A is still guilty of solicitation. If B responds that he will help A, then the offense becomes a conspiracy. A's solicitation merges into a conspiracy that involves both A and B.

2. **Conspiracy.** Conspiracy was a common law misdemeanor and describes a combination by two or more persons to accomplish a criminal or unlawful act, or to do a lawful act by criminal or unlawful means. The generic common law elements of conspiracy are as follows.

   a. ***Actus reus*:** an agreement between two or more persons to act in concert (some jurisdictions also require an overt act, which can be a perfectly legal action, such as buying a map)

   b. ***Mens rea*:** the intent to agree and the intent to commit the underlying offense

   Key to conspiracy law: Protection of society from the dangers of concerted activity and multiple party criminal offenses.

   ***Pinkerton* Rule:** Once a party has joined a conspiracy, liability attaches for acts within the scope and in furtherance of the conspiracy. Also, any acts that are reasonably foreseeable subsequent acts may be included.

   c. Limitations on conspiracy:

      1. **Plurality requirement.** In order to have a conspiracy, an agreement must exist between two or more individuals.

      2. **Wharton's Rule.** If a crime requires the participation of two or more individuals, then it is inappropriate to also charge the parties with the crime of conspiracy. But, the rule does not apply if the number of conspirators exceeds the number essential for the crime.

      3. **Protected Person.** If one of the alleged conspirators is a person who is protected by the law (exempt from prosecution), then that person cannot be a member of the conspiracy.

         Example: A minor victim cannot conspire to commit the crime of statutory rape.

Watch Out!

It is important to remember that conspiracy is a ***separate*** crime. It does ***not*** merge with the completed offense. Thus, conspirators may be prosecuted for both the conspiracy and the underlying crime.

3. Attempt. A common law attempt was a misdemeanor regardless of the nature of the seriousness of the offense that the person sought to commit. Attempts protect against actors who manifest a criminal mind, but whose crime is incomplete.

a. The generic elements of the offense are as follows:

1) ***Mens Rea*:** All attempts are specific intent crimes, even if the attempted offense is a general intent crime. There are two intents:

a) The person must intentionally commit an act; and

b) The person must commit the act with the further intention to commit the target offense (that is, the specific intent).

Watch Out!

Although the completed crime of murder may be satisfied with one of four mental states (intent to kill, intent to cause grievous bodily injury, extreme recklessness/depraved heart, or felony-murder), there is only one mental state that will be sufficient for the crime of **attempted murder**—that is, the **intent to kill.**

2) ***Actus Reus*:** An act beyond mere preparation, into the zone of perpetration.

b. Common law tests for measuring whether the act was beyond preparation include:

1) **Dangerous proximity test** (did the actor come close to completing the crime?)

2) **Probably desistance test** (would the actor have desisted?), and

3) **Equivocality test** (is there another explanation for the behavior?)

c. Model Penal Code uses the **substantial step test** (for incomplete attempts) and requires that the step be strongly corroborative of the actor's criminal intent.

d. **Defenses to Attempt Crimes:**

1) Abandonment

a) **Voluntary abandonment** is recognized by some jurisdictions.

Example: A decides to rob a liquor store. He buys a gun, a ski mask, and gloves to hide his fingerprints. He stakes out the store, looking for the time that the most money will be present and when the owner takes the cash to the bank. He monitors the police activity in the neighborhood and examines the regular customers to determine when they will be present. A wants to rob the store before the owner goes to the bank with the daily cash receipts, but also when the least people will be present. A decides to rob the store one evening. That evening, he puts on his mask and gloves and puts his gun in his pocket. He walks to a location directly across from the store. He walks into the store and just as he is about to pull the gun out and commit the robbery, A feels guilty about this criminal act and walks out without robbing the store. A has voluntarily abandoned the crime. He cannot be convicted of attempted robbery.

b) **Involuntary abandonment** is never a defense.

Example: Same facts. A decides to rob the store another evening. That evening, he puts on his mask and gloves and puts his gun in his pocket. He walks to a location directly across from the store. He walks into the store and just as he is about to pull the gun out and commit the robbery, A sees a police officer parked just outside the store. He decides to commit his robbery another evening, never pulls out his gun, and leaves the store. A is guilty of attempted robbery. He would have robbed the store but for the presence of the police. He involuntarily abandoned the crime.

2) Impossibility

a) **Factual Impossibility** exists when the criminal defendant is unaware of a fact that makes his crime impossible of execution. Factual impossibility is never a defense.

Example: A believes that B, his intended target, is taking a nap in a hammock outside his home. A shoots into the hammock. B is not in the hammock, having gone inside for some iced tea. A is guilty of attempted murder. Factual impossibility is not a defense.

Other examples: Shooting a gun that is not loaded, picking a pocket that is empty.

b) **Legal Impossibility** consists of two types of circumstances:

1) **pure legal impossibility** (which is always a defense). Pure legal impossibility consists of a situation in which the defendant attempts to commit a crime, but his actions (even if fully consummated) would not be a criminal offense.

Example: A believes that it is the crime of rape to touch a woman on the shoulder. A touches a woman on the shoulder. In fact, the law does not consider touching on the shoulder to be rape. This is a case of true legal impossibility and provides a complete defense to the completed offense as well as an attempt to accomplish it.

2) **hybrid legal impossibility**. The better or modern view is that hybrid legal impossibility is ***not*** a defense to an attempt charge. Hybrid legal impossibility consists of a situation in which the defendant makes a mistake of fact relating to a legal status (or attendant circumstance) relevant to the law. Hybrid legal impossibility differs from factual impossibility because the mistake is not simply about any fact, but a fact having legal status or significance.

Example: A receives goods that he believes to have been stolen, but have actually been recovered by the police. In this case, A made a factual mistake about the status of the goods. Notice that the mistake has to do with a legal status relevant to the law—whether the goods are stolen. A is unlikely to have a defense to an attempted receipt of stolen property charge.

Other examples: Attempting to kill a person who is already dead (a live human being is needed for murder), attempting sexual intercourse with a woman who is defendant's wife where the marital immunity applies (a woman not the defendant's wife is needed for rape), shooting a stuffed deer out of season (a live deer needed for deer hunting out of season).

H. LIABILITY FOR THE CONDUCT OF OTHERS

1. Accomplice Liability

Accomplice liability is a method by which unequal participants to a crime are held to be liable for the underlying offense. For instance, the person who is the mastermind behind the robbery of a bank, but is not present during the actual robbery can be held guilty of bank robbery as an accomplice. Accomplice liability is not a separate crime, but one method to hold parties liable for a crime.

The "elements" of accomplice liability are as follows:

Actus Reus: aid in perpetrating the crime; and

Mens Rea: (1) intent to aid and (2) intent that the crime be committed.

a. Common Law Classification of Parties To A Crime (Accomplices):

1) Principals:

a) Principals in the first degree: A principal in the first degree is a person who **actually commits** the crime either by his or her own hand, or by an inanimate agency, or through an innocent human agent.

Example: A commands B to kill X. B kills X by using a revolver. B is a principal in the first degree.

b) Principals in the second degree: A principal in the second degree is a person who is **present** when the crime is committed by another and who aids and abets in its commission but who takes no part in the actual commission of the felony.

Example: A, B, and X are together in each other's presence. A commands B to kill X. B kills X by using a revolver. The felony is committed in A's presence. A is a principal in the second degree. To hold A liable for the death of X as a principal in the second degree, three things must be shown:

i) That B is a guilty principal in the first degree,
ii) That A was present ***actually*** or ***constructively*** when the killing took place, and
iii) That A aided or abetted B in the commission of the felony or that A stood by ready to aid or abet B if necessary. Mere knowledge on A's part that B was to kill X will not make him a party to the crime even if mentally he approves of the crime by B.

2) Accessories:

a) Accessories before the fact: An accessory before the fact is a person who, prior to the commission of the crime, procures, commands or counsels the commission of a felony by another person, but who is **absent** when the felony is committed.

Watch Out!

The main distinction between an **accessory before the fact** and a **principal in the second degree** is that the ***accessory is absent*** and the ***principal is present*** when the crime is committed. **Both** aid and abet the principal in the first degree.

Example: A commands B to kill X. A remains at his home while B goes to X's home and with a revolver kills X. A is an accessory before the fact. To convict A as an accessory before the fact as to X's murder, three things must be shown:
i) That B is a guilty principal in the first degree,
ii) That A was absent at the time of the actual killing, and
iii) That A, prior to the commission of the felony, procured, commanded, counseled, or participated in the preparation for the offense.

Note: Statutes often classify principals in the first degree, principals in the second degree, and accessories before the fact, all as one and the same, and make them liable as principals in the first degree.

b) **Accessories after the fact:** An accessory after the fact is a person who receives, relieves, comforts, or assists another person, with knowledge that the other has committed a felony. Usually, these persons are punished less severely than the other three categories.

Example: B murders X. B then tells A of the murder. A knew nothing of the crime until it was completed by B. A then assists B in disposing of X's body by burying it in a secluded spot. A then hides B in A's house so that he cannot be easily found by the police. A is an accessory after the fact. To convict A as an accessory after the fact, four things must be shown:
i) That a felony had been committed and been complete before A gave any assistance to the felon, B.
ii) That A knew that B had committed the felony.
iii) The accessory must not be guilty of the felony as a principal.
iv) That A rendered assistance or aid to B personally for the purpose of hindering his apprehension or conviction.

3) **Application of Above Rules:**

a) A person may be a principal in the second degree or an accessory before the fact, even though incapable of being a principal in the first degree as to such felony.

Example: Woman, W, commands and counsels man, M, to commit rape on woman X. With the aid of W, man, M, commits rape on woman X. W cannot, because of her sex, commit rape on X as a principal in the first degree (at common law), but may be an accessory before the fact if absent when the rape is committed, or a principal in the second degree if present when the rape is committed.

Note: Today, under modern complicity statutes, W would be an accomplice and would have equal criminal responsibility with M.

b) a person who counsels or commands the commission of a crime is not guilty if he or she repents and countermands the other person before the crime is actually committed.

Example: A commands B to kill X. Before B kills X, A tells B not to commit the crime and that A withdraws from the scheme. B kills X. In this case, A is neither a principal in the second degree nor an accessory before the fact.

b. **Modern Approach to Accomplice Liability.** Many jurisdictions have revised their accomplice liability rules to eliminate the common law classifications discussed above in favor of calling all those who assist the principal an "accomplice." The Model Penal Code § 2.06, Liability for the Conduct of Others, is an example of this approach.

MPC § 2.06 Liability for Conduct of Others:
Under the Model Penal Code, a person is guilty of an offense if it was committed by his own conduct or the conduct of another for which he is legally accountable, or both. A person is accountable for the conduct of another when he is an **accomplice** of the other person in the commission of the offense. A person is an **accomplice** of another person in the commission of the offense if, with the purpose of promoting or facilitating the commission of the offense he:

1) Solicits such person to commit the offense *or*
2) Aids, agrees, or attempts to aid the other person in planning or committing the offense *or*
3) Fails to make proper effort to prevent the commission of the offense when he has a legal duty to do so.

A person is also an accomplice of the person in the commission of the offense when his conduct is expressly declared by law to establish his complicity.

Watch Out!

Equal criminal responsibility exists under modern complicity statutes. The law makes no distinction based upon the amount of participation in the criminal act. If the actor is complicit in the slightest degree, then the actor is responsible for the consequences of the crimes as if he or she had performed the entire crime him or herself.

2. Vicarious Liability

Vicarious liability (the *respondeat superior* rule) is applied under very limited circumstances in the criminal law, largely through statutory law. Vicarious liability imputes the act of one person to another, most often in the employer-employee context. This notion of vicarious liability is at odds with the criminal law's general insistence that liability be personal. A common example of vicarious liability in the criminal law is a statute holding a bar owner responsible for the criminal acts of his employees (the bartenders) in serving liquor to minors.

Watch Out!

Vicarious liability is to be distinguished from strict liability.

Strict liability dispenses with the requirement of *mens rea* (Example: traffic violations have no intent requirements).

In contrast, vicarious liability imputes the criminal act of one person to another. Thus, strict liability is about *mens rea* and vicarious liability is about *actus reus*.

Vicarious liability is also to be distinguished from accessorial liability, which requires proof of an act signifying an intent to join with the original actor as well as co-conspirator liability, which requires proof of an underlying agreement.

3. Corporate Liability for Acts of Employees

a. **General Approach.** The traditional basis for corporate liability for the acts of another is *respondeat superior*. This is the common law test used in federal courts and most state courts.

"A corporation may be held criminally liable for the acts of any of its agents [who] (1) commit a crime (2) within the scope of employment (3) with the intent to benefit the corporation." Under this approach, the type of crime is irrelevant.

b. American Law Institute, Model Penal Code § 2.07(1)(c), Approach:

Minor Offenses (regulatory offenses defined outside the criminal code): Same as the general approach.

Major Offenses (true crimes): A corporation is criminally liable if the criminal conduct was "authorized, requested, commanded, performed or recklessly tolerated by the board of directors or by a high managerial agent acting in behalf of the corporation within the scope of his office or employment."

4. **Conspiratorial Liability**
Recall that not only is conspiracy a separate crime, but it is also a method by which parties are held responsible for the conduct of others. Under the *Pinkerton* rule, conspirators are liable for the act of their co-conspirators that are in furtherance of the conspiracy and within the scope of the conspiracy, or are reasonably foreseeable.

5. **The Crime of Aiding and Abetting.**
The offense of aiding and abetting requires that a person in some way associate him or herself with the criminal venture of another; that he or she participate in it as in something that he wishes to bring about, that he or she seek by his or her action to make it succeed. The generic elements of common law aiding and abetting are as follows.

a. **An act which contributes to the execution of a crime of another** (the *Actus reus*) and,

b. **The intent to aid in its commission** (the *Mens rea*).

Unlike the common law, where accomplice liability is NOT a crime in and of itself, but rather a means of holding unequal participants responsible for the underlying crime—some states and the federal law provide for a separate offense of aiding and abetting. The federal statute follows:

18 USC § 2 Principals
(a) Whoever commits an offense against the United States or aids, abets, counsels, commands, induces or procures its commission, is punishable as a principal.
(b) Whoever willfully causes an act to be done which if directly performed by him or another would be an offense against the United States, is punishable as a principal.

III. AFFIRMATIVE OR TRUE DEFENSES

A. JUSTIFICATION DEFENSES

The focus is on the act. The act is no longer considered unlawful.

1. **Justification.** A justification defense asserts that the existence of one or more objective conditions alters the character of what would otherwise be an unlawful act, changing it from wrong to right. Justifications focus on *the act.*

   Example: A homeowner would affirm the killing of a burglar, but then assert that the threat to the homeowner's life justified or converted what would otherwise be an unlawful act to a lawful act.

2. **Rationale for not punishing justified criminal acts.** Justification defenses address the reality that under certain circumstances, more good (or less harm) comes from breaking the law than obeying it. The corner stone of the doctrine of justification defenses (self defense and necessity) is the necessity to save one's own life **only** at the expense of jettisoning the law. The first rationale of these defenses is the recognition that under circumstances implicating human instinct for survival, the threat of criminal stigma is powerless to modify behavior. A person who faces a life-threatening situation acts on the instinct of survival and neither internal nor external controls can alter this character trait of the human species. Inasmuch as the law is powerless to modify human behavior in a life-threatening situation, there is no role for law to play. Impotency of the law is thus the first, best rationale for the justification and excuse defenses. A second and perhaps more important rationale for withholding the application of law in life threatening situations and that is the observation that even if the law could motivate a behavioral change, it ought not do so where the trade-off decreases good in society. The tragic lifeboat cases present just such a situation. Surely it is preferable that a few die so that many can live, when the alternative is that all die. When faced with the choice between two evils, the law should be flexible to embrace the lesser of the two evils.

3. **Self-defense.** The elements of self-defense are as follows:

   a. **Good faith (subjective) and reasonable belief of** (this is measured by an objective standard)

   b. **Imminent threat of death or serious bodily injury** (to use deadly force)

      Note: The problem with many battered woman's self-defense claims are that they kill their abusers at a time when the threat is not imminent (*e.g.* while their spouse is asleep).

Note: The majority of American jurisdictions do **not** require the person to **retreat** even if it is safe to do so before using deadly force. A minority require retreat ("retreat to the wall") but only when it is safe to do so. In those jurisdictions that require retreat, an exception is made for one's own home.

The **castle doctrine** holds that one is not bound to retreat from his house, even if he may do so with safety to avoid taking the life of an assailant. He may stand his ground and kill the aggressor if it becomes necessary. There is an exception to this rule where the defendant and his attacker share possessory interests in the home.

Example: A is sleeping one evening when he hears a noise downstairs. A quickly gathers his family into second floor bedroom. The bedroom has a fire escape exit that allows for A's quick convenient access to the ground. A looks out his bedroom door and sees a burglar creeping up the stairs with a handgun. A sends his family out of the house via the fire escape. A grabs his own handgun and arms himself. A then walks out of his bedroom and asks the burglar what he thinks he is doing. The burglar tries to shoot A, but A is quicker and shoots and kills the burglar. Because A was in his own home, he can claim self-defense because of the castle doctrine. He has no duty to retreat even though he safely could.

c. **The defendant does not escalate the level of force**, and

d. **The defendant is not the initial aggressor**.

Note: The mitigation of imperfect self-defense may be available to reduce murder to voluntary manslaughter if a perfect self-defense claim fails.

4. **Defense of others.** One may use reasonable force in defense of another subject to the following:

   a. **The majority rule is that one who intervenes in a struggle between strangers under the mistaken, but reasonable belief, that he is protecting another who he assumes is being unlawfully beaten is thereby exonerated from criminal liability**.

   b. **The minority rule is that one who goes to the aid of a third person does so at his own peril**. The settled policy of law in some jurisdictions is that the right of a person to defend another ordinarily should be no greater than such person's right to defend himself.

   Example: A intervenes to help B in a fight with C. Unbeknownst to A, the intervener, C, the perceived attacker, is actually an undercover police officer. However, A reasonably believes that C is a wrongdoer. Under the majority rule, A would be acquitted based upon a reasonable mistake. Under the minority rule, A, the intervener, will be guilty of interfering with a police officer.

5. **Defense of habitation.** This privilege permits one to take the life of an intending trespasser, if the dweller reasonably believes that the threatened entry is for the purpose of committing a felony or inflicting great bodily harm upon an occupant of the house. The rule is even broader in some jurisdictions, allowing the occupant to prevent an intrusion, the apparent purpose of which is an assault or other violence non-felonious in nature.

   a. **Rationale for the rule.** The defense of habitation against a dangerous intruder is a right which stems from the law's early view that a man's home is his "fortress" or "castle."

   b. **Deadly force versus non-deadly force.** The right to defend the habitation permits one to use non-deadly force to prevent a mere civil trespass, although it does not countenance the use of a deadly force for that purpose. Where deadly force is inflicted upon a trespasser, however, aggravating circumstances of the trespass may constitute such provocation to make the killing manslaughter, rather than murder. The defense of property rides piggyback to the defense of self and others, and thus deadly force may not be employed in the defense of mere property where no one is present.

      Example: A sets a trap to foil would-be burglars by strategically positioning a spring gun to fire at the rear doorway of his business. A then goes on vacation leaving the premises vacant. If a burglar trips the spring gun and is thereby killed, A would be exposed to liability for homicide.

   c. **Extension of the rule to household occupants other than the owner.** The rule allows defense of the habitation by guests or servants of the household, where the occupant himself would be justified in making a defense.

   d. **Extension of the rule to defense of business premises.** Defense of habitation has been held to encompass the protection of one's place of business, in addition to his dwelling.

6. **Defense of property.** A person is justified in the use of reasonable force to prevent or terminate criminal interference with his or her possessions or other right in property subject to the following limitations

   a. The use of force at criminal levels must be in immediate response to interference with property rights and in the presence of the property owner.

   b. The use of deadly force is never justified in the defense of property. Human life is the prime value recognized in the criminal law, and the law places a higher value on the life of a wrongdoer than property. The only cases in which the defendant is apparently justified in the use of deadly force while protecting property are those cases where the defendant is actually in his home defending himself and otherwise meets the elements of self-defense.

7. **Law enforcement and resisting arrest.** A police officer, or a person aiding him, is justified in using reasonable force to make a lawful arrest or to prevent the escape from custody of one already arrested.

   a. **Misdemeanors.** Deadly force may not be used to arrest or prevent the escape of a misdemeanant.

   b. **Felonies.** Deadly force may be used in the case of a felon if it reasonably appears that the felon will otherwise avoid arrest or escape from custody.

      An officer may use deadly force if he reasonably perceives a threat to the officer's personal safety or to innocent bystanders.

8. **Necessity.**
   A necessity defense can be raised when a person faces the difficult choice between abiding by the law and suffering a great harm or breaking the law and suffering a lesser harm. Sometimes, this defense is known as "the choice of evils" defense. Traditionally, the conditions requiring the choice of evils must come from the physical forces of nature rather than human beings. If the pressure comes from human beings, the appropriate defense is duress (see below under excuses defenses).

   Example: A is caught in an unexpected blizzard on the top of a mountain and burglarizes B's home to take shelter.

   Example: A burns B's field of corn to prevent a forest fire from spreading to a small town and killing the inhabitants.

   Please note: **Necessity is probably no defense to murder.** In an old English case involving sailors in a lifeboat, the court held that it was murder for the three sailors to kill and eat the cabin boy. In an American case involving crew members and passengers in a lifeboat, the court upheld a manslaughter conviction for throwing some passengers overboard and stated that lots should have be drawn. This is an area of some controversy and debate.

   a. **Elements of necessity.** The elements of the defense of necessity are as follows:

      1) an imminent threat of death or serious bodily injury (usually from a force of nature);

      2) actor reasonably believes action will abate harm;

3) harm caused by actor is less than harm avoided ("choice of evils");

4) no legal alternative exists;

5) the legislature has not spoken on the choice of evils; and

6) the actor has clean hands (the actor was not at fault).

b. **Necessity distinguished from duress.** Necessity applies where the threat owes to a force of nature; duress applies where the threat owes to a human actor. Necessity is evaluated on an objective standard; duress is evaluated on a subjective standard.

Example: Two persons, who owe no duty to one another that is not mutual, should by accident, not attributable to either, be placed in a situation where both cannot survive neither would commit a crime in saving his own life in a struggle for the only means of safety. A and B are on a luxury cruise in the middle of the ocean. The boat sinks and both are thrown into the water. At the same time, both see a single life vest floating in the water. No other means of survival is present. Both A and B swim for the vest and a struggle ensues over the vest with both parties kicking and punching each other. A wins the struggle, B drowns, and A is charged with the murder of B. A will prevail on a defense of necessity.

9. **Imperfect justification.** Because excuse defenses speak to subjectively human frailty as opposed to objective justification, there is an "imperfect analog" to any justification defense. Thus, where the actor subjectively mistakenly believes that he has met the elements of any justification defense or where the actor is otherwise excused from meeting all of the elements of a justification defense because of his personal limitations, he may assert the imperfect justification defense as an excuse.

Example: A battered wife who fails the requirements of perfect self defense may nevertheless argue that she did her best under the imperfect defense of self-defense. The argument might go as follows:

a. Although her sleeping husband did not objectively present an imminent threat, she perceived him to be a threat whenever he was awake,

b. Although there was an avenue of escape available to her, she does not perceive that leaving home is a viable option,

c. Although she escalates the level of force by returning gun play for fisticuffs, she perceives the gun to be a necessary equalizer given the disparity in his size and his violent nature,

d. Although she is the initial aggressor, she believes she has no chance without getting the jump on him and cannot reasonable attack him when he is awake.

B. EXCUSE DEFENSES

The focus is on the actor. The act is still considered illegal, but we excuse the actor because of some condition.

1. **Excuse.** In contrast, an excuse defense asserts that the existence of one or more conditions personal to the actor alters his personal responsibility for the otherwise criminal act. Excuses focus on *the actor* (the act is still unlawful).

   Example: A could affirm his role as a "mule" in drug trafficking but argue that the threat to his life from a higher up excused his wrongful conduct or makes punishment unfair.

2. **Rationale for reducing punishment for excused criminal acts.** In contrast, excuse addresses the reality of human frailty and under certain circumstances authorizes the reduction of punishment or its withholding altogether when human actors fall short of the requirements of law. Excuse (provocation and duress) is a broader doctrine than justification in that excuse allows the jury to take into account the actor's physical and mental deficiencies to lower the standard by which to judge him; in excuse the act is wrong, but not punishable. Only after the initial choice is made to violate the law by an individual, does excuse provide a role for law; that role being to evaluate and approve or disapprove the initial choice made by the individual. The common law applied excuse defenses strictly because assessing individual bias is inherently determinative. However, modern common law has been more accommodating to tribal bias as seen by the widespread acceptance of syndrome evidence.

3. **Distinguishing justification from excuse.** Perhaps the easiest way to appreciate the distinction between justification and excuse is to analyze the role of an aider or abettor to the principal actor. In the case of justification, the innocence of the aider and abettor follows lockstep with the principal actor: if the principal actor is justified, the act is lawful and aiders and abettors are innocent. In contrast, in the case of excuse, the aider or abettor can never be innocent, since the defendant's act is wrongful: the principal actor has a personal defense given human frailty; not so for aiders and abettors.

   Example of justification: A Good Samaritan who aids an Actor in an altercation is innocent of wrongdoing, if the actor is justified under a claim of self-defense.

   Example of excuse: Suppose the victim of a car accident climbs out of the wreck and clubs the drunk driver out of grief or revenge for the death of his family. The law will personally excuse, at least partially, this Actor under a claim of provocation. However, an aider or abettor who joins in the clubbing will have no such defense.

4. **Duress.**

   a. **Elements.** The elements of duress are as follows:

      1) That there be a threat that an accused or an innocent person be immediately killed or seriously injured; and

      2) That there be a reasonable apprehension that the threat will be carried out and that apprehension continue throughout the commission of the offense; and

      3) That there is no reasonable opportunity to avoid committing the act; and

      4) That the person was not at fault in exposing himself to the threat.

   b. **Duress is not a defense to murder.** The majority rule is that duress is not a defense to murder. The rationale is that the defendant is not allowed to trade a higher act in exchange for a lower act and is not allowed to trade a life at all. Duress is rarely successful as a defense because it requires the claimant to demonstrate a high level of courage before resorting to a criminal act.

      Example: At common law, as opposed to drawing his gun and killing his approaching attacker, a hemophiliac should accept a slap, even if the slap risks the occurrence of a bleeding injury, and even at the outside risk that such bleeding might lead to death. The innocent human actor should accept a risk of death over certain death even as to a wrongdoer.

5. **Insanity.**

   a. **Insanity Generally:** the Insanity defense is an affirmative defense in which the law makes a special classification of individuals, excusing conduct on their part which would otherwise be criminal because of their capacity to understand their actions. Today, insanity is not an absolute acquittal. A jury will return a verdict of not guilty by reason of insanity as distinguished from a complete acquittal of not guilty. An actor found not guilty by reason of insanity is not released, but stays under the control of the court. Insanity governs the actor at the time of the act. Competency to stand trial governs the actor at the time of the trial and focuses on the actor's current ability to appreciate the criminal proceedings and assist his attorney with his defense.

   b. **Different Tests for Insanity:**

      1) **The *M'Naghten* Test.** The *M'Naghten* rule is the insanity test used in the majority of American jurisdictions. It is a purely cognitive test. The *M'Naghten* Rule defines insanity by evaluating at the time of committing of the act, whether the party accused was laboring under such a defect of

reason, from disease of the mind, as not to know the nature and quality of the act he was doing; or, if he did know it, that he did not know he was doing what was wrong.

Elements of the *M'Naghten* test for insanity are:
Whether the defendant was laboring under such a defect of reason, from disease of the mind,
(a) as to not know the nature and quality of the act he was doing; or
(b) if he did know it, he did not know he was doing what was wrong.

a) **The party must labor under a defect of reason from a disease of the mind.**

Few courts have actually defined what constitutes a disease of the mind, but any mental abnormality or deficiency that causes the results in the second portion of the test will suffice. The law does not say what specific mental abnormalities are necessary to satisfy the requirement of a disease of the mind, but the actor must have a substantial, definable condition, not a borderline one caused by limited intelligence.

b) **That prevents him from understanding at the time of the criminal act either, not both, of the below criteria:**

1. **The nature and quality of the act.** The nature and quality of the act is an analysis of whether or not the actor can appreciate the significance of his actions.

2. **Knowledge as to the moral/legal wrongness of his actions**. This prong considers whether or not the defendant had the ability to understand right from wrong.

In the case where a person is under a delusion, the evaluation of such a delusion turns on what is the nature of the delusion. A delusion that a killing is necessary for self-defense is a defense, while a delusion to exact revenge for an inadequate provocation is not.

Example of *M'Naghten:* A has a huge brain tumor that has filled 75% of his skull. As a result of the pressure on his brain from this tumor, A cannot always perceive the events around him clearly and often distorts reality because he believes that his TV speaks to him. A also does whatever his TV asks him to do. One day, A takes a gun and starts shooting people in the street. A believes that he is shooting pigeons and that his TV wants him to kill pigeons. Clearly, A has a defect in reason brought on by a disease of the mind. A's brain tumor and the pressure on his brain from this tumor cause him to distort reality and not understand that he is actually shooting people. Lastly, because he sincerely believes he is doing his TV's will, he cannot appreciate the wrongfulness of his actions. Using *M'Naghten,* A would be found not guilty by reason of insanity.

2) **The Irresistible Impulse Test.** (This is a minority view). A few jurisdictions that use the purely cognitive *M'Naghten* insanity test supplement it with the irresistible impulse test, a volitional test that focuses on the defendant's loss of control.

In short, the analysis focuses on whether the defendant had a mental disease that prevented him from controlling his actions.

Example of the Irresistible Impulse Test: A has a huge brain tumor that has filled 75% of his skull. As a result of the pressure on his brain from this tumor, A cannot always perceive the events around him clearly and often distorts reality because he believes that his TV speaks to him. A also does whatever his TV asks him to do. One day, A takes a gun and starts shooting at people in the street. A believes that the TV wants him to kill people and that he has been chosen for this task. A cannot stop himself as, while he is shooting, he hears the TV encouraging him to shoot more and more people. In this case, A's actions are the result of a mental disorder that prevents him from controlling his actions. A may know that killing another human being is wrong, but will not stop because he cannot control his actions.

3) **The Product or *Durham* Test.** The recognition that insanity is a complex phenomenon led to recognition of the Product test. This test permits a jury to find a defendant not guilty if it believes beyond a reasonable doubt that the accused suffered from a mental disease or defect and that there was sufficient causal connection between the mental abnormality and the accused's unlawful act to excuse the defendant from criminal responsibility for it.

The *Durham* product test excuses a criminal act that is the product of a mental disease or defect.

Example of the Product Test: A has a huge brain tumor that has filled 75% of his skull. As a result of the pressure on his brain from this tumor, A cannot always perceive the events around him clearly and often distorts reality because he believes that his TV speaks to him. One day, A takes a gun and starts shooting at people in the street. A believes that his TV wants him to kill people and that he has been chosen for this task. A cannot stop himself as, while he is shooting, he hears his TV encouraging him to shoot more and more people. A's actions are clearly the "product" of his brain tumor and he will be found not guilty by reason of insanity because of the Product test.

4) **The American Law Institute (ALI)/Model Penal Code (MPC) Test.** A significant minority of American jurisdictions follow the Model Penal Code test for insanity. The test has both cognitive and volitional prongs. It rejects the traditional *M'Naghten* test as not keeping pace with the modern day advancements in medical science.

> Elements of the ALI/MPC test for insanity are:
>
> As a result of a mental disease or defect,
>
> (a) the person lacks substantial capacity to appreciate the wrongfulness of his conduct, or
>
> (b) the person lacks substantial capacity to conform his conduct to the requirements of the law.

The ALI test only requires that the actor lack substantial capacity. A mental disease or defect includes any abnormal condition of the mind which substantially affects mental or emotional processes and substantially affects behavior controls. The Model Penal Code Test is both a cognitive and a volitional test. Federal jurisdictions used the complete MPC Test until Congress passed the Insanity Defense Reform Act, which eliminated the second prong.

Example of the ALI Test: A has a huge brain tumor that has filled 75% of his skull. As a result of the pressure on his brain from this tumor, A cannot always perceive the events around him clearly and often distorts reality because he believes that his TV speaks to him. However, A has very lucid days as well. One day, A takes a gun and starts shooting at people in the street. A believes that his TV wants him to kill people and that he has been chosen for this task. A cannot stop himself as, while he is shooting, he hears his TV encouraging him to shoot more and more people. A will be found not guilty by reason of insanity because at the time of his actions, because of his tumor, he lacked the substantial capacity to appreciate the wrongfulness of his actions. A has lucid days, but at the time he was under the control of his TV, his mental defect prevented him from understanding his actions.

C. TRADITIONAL THEORIES OF PUNISHMENT

1. **Restraint** (sometimes called incapacitation). Restraint operates on the theory that we must restrain or incapacitate a criminal from committing future wrongs by placing that person in prison.

2. **Specific Deterrence** (sometimes called prevention). Specific Deterrence is aimed at deterring an individual (rather than others) from committing future crimes by providing an unpleasant experience that will decrease the chances of that person committing another crime.

3. **General Deterrence.** The theory of general deterrence is that if we punish an individual for committing a crime, this will decrease the chances of other committing the same crime because they do not want to suffer the same fate.

4. **Denunciation.** Denunciation justifies punishment of behavior where society has no purpose other than to show its repugnance at the activity brought to light. This justification has application, for example in the lifeboat scenario where a person is killed and eaten to sustain the lives of the remaining survivors. The underlying rationale for imposing punishment in these cases is to reduce the inherent human temptation to give short shrift to social costs. Denunciation serves this purpose by reinforcing moral principles and maintaining a cost to disobedience.

5. **Retribution** (sometimes called revenge or retaliation). Quite similar to denunciation, retribution justifies punishment simply on the ground that a crime was committed. Future benefits, if any are incidental. However, unlike the denunciation justification, the rationale of retribution is that the offender owes a debt to society; punishment is the mode of repayment. Retribution contains an element of proportionality by embracing the principle of *Lex talionis*, *i.e.,* punishment should exact the same injury inflicted (popularly expressed in Hammarabi's code: as an eye for an eye, tooth for a tooth).

6. **Rehabilitation** (sometimes called reformation). Rehabilitation advocates recommend a healing or medical vice punitive response to crime. Rehabilitation thus employs corrective techniques to make the offender more law-abiding, such techniques may theoretically be exercised until they have succeeded; and thus sentencing can be as long as necessary. It is also argued that rehabilitation, not punishment makes sense because when enough is sympathetically understood about a person, blaming becomes impossible, even in the case of the person who commits atrocities or is utterly selfish. Psychiatry offers the promise of correcting antisocial behavior through the manipulation of the individual psyche and begins with motivating or stimulating or arousing in a cornered individual the wish and hope and intention to change his methods of dealing with the realities of life. In addition to treatment modalities, facilitation such as new job opportunities, vacation trips, *etc*., contribute to a total treatment effect.

IV. BASIC CONSTITUTIONAL DUE PROCESS

A. THE *WINSHIP* DOCTRINE

1. **Presumption of innocence.** The "presumption of innocence" is a procedural device used to increase the probability that any unknowing error made in the final outcome of a criminal trial favors the liberty interest of the accused over the security interest of the community. The presumption of innocence applies to the trial on the merits, but not at pretrial hearings such as bail hearings, competency inquiries, motions to suppress, etc.

2. **Proof beyond a reasonable doubt.** As the "presumption of innocence" operates to favor the possible error of a wrongful acquittal over a wrongful conviction, the margin of error is established by the burden of proof to convict, which in criminal cases is proof beyond a reasonable doubt. The proof beyond a reasonable doubt standard adopted ***In re Winship*** protects an accused against conviction in a criminal trial except upon proof beyond a reasonable doubt of every element necessary to constitute the crime charged.

3. **Presumptions and inferences:** Presumptions and inferences refer to the same logical devices that permit the prosecution to indirectly prove an elemental fact or factual ingredient of the crime by direct proof or circumstantial evidence. There are permissive and mandatory inferences, and a second divide of rebuttable and mandatory inferences.

   a. **Constitutional standards for permissive inferences.** Permissive inferences comport with the "beyond a reasonable doubt standard" established in ***Winship*** if, under the facts of the case, there is a "rational connection" between the fact proven and the fact presumed. Under ***Leary v. United States*,** a "rational connection" means that the presumed fact is more likely than not to flow from the proved fact on which it is made to depend.

      Example: The police stop a car containing four persons and a gun located in an open console between the driver and the front passenger seat. The presence of the gun within eyesight and arm's length permits an inference that all four occupants of the car possessed the gun.

   b. **Mandatory presumptions which shift the burden of persuasion are unconstitutional.** Mandatory presumptions may be either conclusive or rebuttable. A conclusive presumption removes the presumed element from the case once the State has proven the predicate facts giving rise to the presumption. A rebuttable presumption does not remove the presumed element from the case but nevertheless requires the jury to find the presumed element unless the defendant persuades the fact finder that such a finding is unwarranted. A mandatory conclusive presumption, which shifts the burden of production necessarily, also shifts the burden of persuasion onto the defendant because of its mandatory and conclusive nature and accordingly they are not generally acceptable under ***Winship***.

Example: It is constitutionally impermissible to infer that A intended to murder B merely from the commission of a homicidal act.

c. **Mandatory presumptions which merely shift the burden of production are constitutional.** Mandatory rebuttable presumptions, which merely shift the burden of production to the defendant, while leaving the ultimate burden of persuasion on the prosecution are acceptable under ***Winship***.

Example: It is constitutionally permissible that the intoxication part of the offense of driving can be established by a level of blood alcohol content at 10%.

Example: A shift in the burden of proof to the defendant for an insanity defense is constitutional as well.

B. PROCEDURAL BURDENS AT TRIAL

1. **Burdens of pleading.**
The burden of pleading identifies the party at trial on whom is placed the initial obligation to notify the opposing party and the court what legal claim is being asserted in question and, if applicable, what particular variation of the crime is under contention. The burden of pleading is thus a notice requirement as to minor discrepancies, but jurisdictional as to major discrepancies between pleading and practice.

a. **Government's burden of pleading.** The government's burden of pleading is met when the charge sheet describes the crime in sufficient factual detail and with sufficient elemental accuracy to fairly place the defendant on notice as to what the charge is so that a defense may be prepared. The procedural effect of a failure of the government to meet its burden of pleading depends on the stage of the proceeding. The government may amend before trial or during trial if the pleading error is minor. Dismissal is the only remedy for a major pleading error discovered at trial or after the trial. Unless the misspecification is related to an insufficiency of evidence, the Court will usually dismiss without prejudice, which means the government is free to re-try the accused on the same underlying acts constituting the offense.

b. **Defendant's burden of pleading.** The defendant rarely is assigned a burden of pleading, since notice to the government would ease the government's burden to prove all elements of the crime charged by limiting the matters in controversy prior to the government meeting its burden to establish a *prima facie* case. However, as a matter of judicial economy, most jurisdictions permit two exceptions to this general rule in cases involving the defense of insanity or alibi, which if provable, are fairly dispositive of guilt in advance of trial.

2. **Burden of production.** The burden of production identifies the party at trial on whom is placed the initial obligation to provide factual evidence to support the legal claim being asserted. The burden of production is sometimes described as the burden of raising sufficient evidence to place an issue in controversy or to require a response from the opposition.

   a. **The government's production burden.** The government bears the burden of producing evidence on the elements of the crime charged. The quantum of evidence required to meet the government's production burden is preponderance of the evidence. The government's production burden is met when the government produces credible evidence on each element of the offense charged and when done constitutes the government's *prima facie* case. The failure of the government to meet its production burden results in a directed verdict of dismissal.

   b. **The defense's production burden.** Negative defenses comprise defense claims at trial that the facts may tend to negate an element of the crime. In contrast, affirmative defenses comprise defense claims at trial which affirm that the elements of the crime have been made out, but argue that the criminal sanction should not apply due to the existence of a fact or circumstance which allegedly brings the charged behavior back into the realm of normal or at least non-criminal behavior. The defense bears the burden of production solely for affirmative defenses or true defenses which refer to a fact or circumstance that is not an explicit part of the definition of the crime or an ingredient of the elements of the crime, such as alibi and insanity, and not for negative defenses.

      Example: The defense of voluntary intoxication is a negative defense and may support a claim negating the *mens rea* in the case of specific intent (common law) or purpose and knowing (Model Penal Code) crimes, or even *actus reus* in the case of severe, prolonged drunkenness. However, if the claim is that defendant's drunkenness is severe and for extended periods of time, the evidence might support a claim of insanity or temporary insanity, and as such the defense may functionally operate as an affirmative defense in that the defendant would bear a burden or pleading and production to raise and commit the alcohol induced insanity defense into controversy.

   c. **Quantum of evidence needed to meet the defendant's burden of proof.** The quantum of evidence required to meet the defendant's burden of production concerning an affirmative defense varies according to jurisdiction. Some jurisdictions require a "preponderance of the evidence," others allow for a mere "scintilla of evidence," still others strike some middle ground betwixt and between allowing that 'some evidence' will suffice. The procedural effect of the defense meeting its production burden is the benefit of a jury instruction to consider the defense regardless of the government's rebuttal, since whether the rebuttal is successful is a jury question.

d. **Government's burden to rebut affirmative defenses.** Once the affirmative defense is successfully raised, the quantum of evidence which is required of the government to disprove the defense is proof beyond a reasonable doubt.

3. **Burdens of persuasion.** The burden of persuasion is a rule, which determines who bears the obligation to convince the jury of the accuracy of an asserted factual claim, *i.e.*, which party bears the risk of failing to convince the jury that its factual claim is true.

a. **Government's burden of persuasion.** The government bears the burden of persuasion for each element of the offense as charged, including any special facts or implicit ingredients constituting the offense. In addition, the government assumes the burden of persuasion to disprove any negative defenses raised either by the government's evidence or affirmative defenses introduced by the defense. The quantum of evidence required to meet the government's burden of persuasion is proof beyond a reasonable doubt.

b. **The defense burden of persuasion.** As a general rule, the defense does not have a burden of persuasion. However, some commentators have argued that the quantum of evidence needed to raise the defense of insanity makes the production burden to raise this defense functionally equivalent to a burden of persuasion.

C. STANDARD OF PROOF AT SENTENCING

1. **Beyond degrees of guilt to character of the accused.** The law of crimes is not only concerned with the ultimate question of guilt or innocence, but also with degrees of guilt. Punishment should be proportional to the degree of guilt. A criminal trial is bifurcated into two mini trials. In the guilt phase, guilt and the degree of guilt are determined. In the penalty phase, the character of the accused and the magnitude of harm caused are determined. The prosecution bears the burden of persuasion at the guilt phase, and this burden must meet the reasonable doubt standard. In contrast, at the penalty phase, neither party bears the burden of persuasion and the burden of production only serves to order the presentation of evidence.

2. **Aggravated offenses and aggravating sentencing factors.** The ***Winship*** doctrine is implicated in two ways in defining the substantive crime.

a. **Aggravated offenses with more easily provable mental states.** First, the legislature can statutorily reconfigure a crime so as to make hard to prove elements "attendant circumstances" with lower associated mental states, if any. For example, an aggravated form of battery is battery on a police officer. If the police officer is working under cover and the defendant does not know the victim is a police officer, the legislature can make the absence of knowledge concerning the victim's status an "attendant circumstance" irrelevant as long as the defendant knew he was committing an unlawful battery.

b. **Re-casting aggravation elements as sentencing factors which do not bear a burden of proof.** Second, the legislature can define a basic offense and shift all forms of aggravation to sentencing where the prosecutor need only establish their proof on a preponderance standard. For example, the use of a weapon, recidivism, drugs, or special interest protection are aggravating factors, which may be shifted to sentencing factors only. The ability of the legislature to ease the prosecution's burden of proof by redefining aggravation factors as sentencing factors and thus shifting proof of such factors from the strict requirements at trial where the prosecution generally bears all aspects of the burden of proof except for producing evidence of affirmative offenses to the relaxed standards at sentencing where neither party bears the burden of persuasion has made for increasingly complex questions of procedure

Basic rule concerning sentencing factors. The legislature may insulate aggravating factors from the due process requirements of ***Winship***, and thus re-cast aggravating factors as sentencing factors so long as the sentencing factors only increase the mandatory minimum sentence or generate a harsher sentence within the original range of the base offense. However, if the sentencing factors have the effect of increasing the maximum permissible sentence of the base offense, such a legislative formulation violates due process and such aggravating sentencing factors must be pled and proven beyond a reasonable doubt at trial. The trier of fact must make that specific finding.

3. **Standards of proof at death penalty cases:** Death penalty cases are bifurcated into the eligibility phase and selection phase. In the eligibility phase, the jury narrows the class of defendants eligible for the death penalty, often through consideration of aggravating circumstances. In the selection phase, the jury determines whether to impose a death sentence on an eligible defendant.

a. **Eligibility (or Guilt) phase.** In the eligibility, or guilt phase the Court has stressed the need for channeling and limiting the jury's discretion to ensure that the death penalty is a proportionate punishment and therefore not arbitrary or capricious in its imposition.

b. Selection (or Penalty) phase. By contrast in the selection, or penalty, phase, the Court has emphasized the need for a broad inquiry into all relevant mitigating evidence to allow an individualized determination. The Court has determined that in the sentencing phase, the sentencing body may not be precluded from considering, and may not refuse to consider, any constitutionally relevant mitigating evidence.

D. STANDARDS OF APPELLATE REVIEW

1. **Sufficiency of the evidence.** The standard of review for an appeal on the basis of sufficiency of the evidence requires that the resolution of factual disputes and all reasonable inferences from the proven facts are to be construed against the moving party on appeal. Except for appeal *de novo*, an appellate court is usually limited to reviewing matters of law, not evidence. Thus, the reviewing court must construe the facts and logical inferences flowing there from in a manner consistent with the verdict at trial. Therefore, in analyzing cases post-conviction, the factual conflicts and ambiguities are to be reasonably construed in favor of the conviction which the jury returned. Accordingly, except for government appeals, the prosecution and defendant reverse roles on appeal. In appealing a conviction, the defendant now carries the burden to establish an error in law (most appellate jurisdictions are limited to reviewing errors of law).

2. **Defenses not raised at trial.** If the error assigned is insufficiency of the evidence, the possible errors may actually comprehend specific defenses, the validity of which an appellate court is free to evaluate on appeal.

V. CONSTITUTIONAL DEFENSES

A. FAIR WARNING

There are three related manifestations of the fair warning requirement. These are void-for-vagueness, lenity, and notice.

1. **Void-for-vagueness.** The vagueness doctrine bars enforcement of a statute which either forbids or requires the doing of an act in terms so vague that men of common intelligence must necessarily guess at its meaning and differ as to its application. The void-for-vagueness doctrine requires that a penal statute define the criminal offense with sufficient definiteness that ordinary people can understand what conduct is prohibited, and in a manner that does not encourage arbitrary and discriminatory enforcement.

2. **Rule of lenity.** Lenity ensures fair warning to putative defendants by so resolving ambiguity in a criminal statute as to apply it only to conduct clearly covered. The rule that penal laws are to be construed strictly is founded on the tenderness of the law for the rights of individuals; and on the plain principle that the power of punishment is vested in the legislative, not in the judicial department (the principle of legality). The rule of lenity, applies not only to interpretations of the substantive ambit of criminal prohibitions, but also to the penalties they impose. Though lenity is usually invoked when there is doubt about whether a legislature has criminalized particular conduct, lenity also means that the Court will not

interpret a federal criminal statute so as to increase the penalty that it places on an individual when such an interpretation can be based on no more than a guess as to what Congress intended. It may fairly be said to be a presupposition of American penal statutes to resolve doubts in the enforcement of a penal code against the imposition of harsher punishment.

3. **Notice.** Third, although clarity at the requisite level may be supplied by judicial gloss on an otherwise uncertain statute, due process bars courts from applying a novel construction of a criminal statute to conduct that neither the statute nor any prior judicial decision has fairly disclosed to be within its scope.

B. CANONS OF CONSTRUCTION

1. ***Mens rea.*** Where a criminal statute is silent as to any scienter requirement, the canon of statutory interpretation is to presume an implicit requirement of scienter in the absence of express statutory intent to the contrary. The presumed intent is general intent.

2. ***Actus Reus.*** Congressional silence in omitting an overt act requirement to drug trafficking conspiracy laws shall be honored as valid legislative intent.

C. EX POST FACTO LAWS

1. **Constitutional prohibition.** Article I, §10 of the Federal Constitution provides that "no State shall . . . pass any . . . ex post facto Law." The constitutional prohibition and the judicial interpretation of the ex post facto clause rests upon the notion that laws, whatever their form, which purport to make innocent acts criminal after the event, or to aggravate an offense, are harsh and oppressive, and that the criminal quality attributable to an act, either by the legal definition of the offense or by the nature or amount of the punishment imposed for its commission, should not be altered by legislative enactment, after the fact, to the disadvantage of the accused.

2. ***Ex post facto* clause applies to re-defining crimes or increases in punishment after the fact.** The Ex post facto clause prohibits laws that retroactively alter the definition of crimes or increase the punishment for criminal acts.

   Example: A likes to fish. A has fished every day in Winding Creek for the last 10 years. The state legislature, in an attempt to set up a wildlife preserve, bans all fishing in Winding Creek from January 1, 2004 onward. Further, the statute also empowers the local prosecuting attorney to charge people who had fished in Winding Creek within the last ten years. The local prosecutor charges A with violating the state statute because he fished in Winding Creek. The law would be struck down as a violation of the *ex post facto* clause.

Example: A is in prison for murder. His sentence is 25 years and he has served 20 years. The state legislature, in an effort to become tough on crime, makes the penalty for murder 50 years. A does not have to serve the additional time because such a penalty would be a violation of the *ex post facto* clause.

Printed in Dunstable, United Kingdom

91218875R00045